A Brave New Quest

Middle East Literature in Translation

Michael Beard *and* Adnan Haydar, *Series Editors*

Other titles in the Middle East Literature in Translation series

A Child from the Village
Sayyid Qutb; John Calvert and William Shepard, ed. and trans.

The Committee
Sonallah Ibrahim; Mary St. Germain and Charlene Constable, trans.

A Cup of Sin: Selected Poems
Simin Behbahani; Farzaneh Milani and Kaveh Safa, trans.

Granada
Radwa Ashour; William Granara, trans.

In Search of Walid Masoud: A Novel
Jabra Ibrahim Jabra; Roger Allen and Adnan Haydar, trans.

The Night of the First Billion
Ghada Samman; Nancy N. Roberts, trans.

Nightingales and Pleasure Gardens: Turkish Love Poems
Talat S. Halman, ed. and trans.; Jayne L. Warner, assoc. ed.

Sleeping in the Forest: Stories and Poems
Sait Faik; Talat S. Halman, ed.; Jayne L. Warner, assoc. ed.

Three Tales of Love and Death
Out el Kouloub

A Time Between Ashes and Roses
Adonis; Shawkut M. Toorawa, ed. and trans.

Women Without Men: A Novella
Shahrnush Parsipur; Kamran Talattof and Jocelyn Sharlet, trans.

Zanouba: A Novel.
Out el Kouloub; Nayra Atiya, trans.

A Brave New Quest

100 Modern Turkish Poems

Editor and Translator

Talat S. Halman

Associate Editor

Jayne L. Warner

S|U

Syracuse University Press

English translations copyright © 2006 by Syracuse University Press
Syracuse, New York 13244–5160
All Rights Reserved

First Edition 2006
06 07 08 09 10 11 6 5 4 3 2 1

Illustrations: Detail from İznik tile in the Rüstem Pasha Mosque (1561), Istanbul. The mosque was built in honor of Rüstem Pasha, a grand vizier and son-in-law of Sultan Süleyman the Magnificent. From *The Book of Rüstem Paşa Tiles,* Fatih Cimok, ed., Suat Eman, photographer (Istanbul: A. Turizm Yayınları, 1998), p. 14. Courtesy of the publisher.

The paper used in this publication meets the minimum requirements of American National Standard for Information Science—Permanence of Paper for Printed Library Materials, ANSI Z39.48–1984.

Library of Congress Cataloging-in-Publication Data
A brave new quest : 100 modern Turkish poems / editor and translator, Talat S. Halman ;
associate editor, Jayne L. Warner.
p. cm.—(Middle East literature in translation)
Includes bibliographical references (p.).
ISBN 0–8156–0840–3 (pbk. only : alk. paper)
1. Turkish poetry—Translations into English. I. Halman, Talât Sait.
II. Warner, Jayne L. III. Series.
PL232 .B 73 2005
894'.351008—dc22
2005032788

Manufactured in the United States of America

Contents

Preface *xi*
Note on Turkish Spelling *xv*

Ahmet Hamdi Tanpınar Fear *3*
Awakening *4*

Nazım Hikmet Today Is Sunday *5*
Silence *6*
From: The Epic of the War of Liberation *8*
From: The Epic of Sheikh Bedreddin *10*
Quatrains *15*
About Living *17*
[untitled] *20*
No Tree Has Ever Given Such Marvelous Fruit *21*

Necip Fazıl Kısakürek Anguish *22*

Asaf Halet Çelebi Abraham *27*

Ahmet Muhip Dıranas Two Solitary Trees *28*

Cahit Sıtkı Tarancı Poem at Thirty-Five *29*
After Death *31*
Terror *32*

Bedri Rahmi Eyuboğlu The Saga of Istanbul *33*

Fazıl Hüsnü Dağlarca | *From: The Epic of Çakır* 40
In Passage 41
Ugly 42
From: The Epic of the Conquest of Istanbul 45
Stone Inscription 48
To the Public Prosecutor 49
Quatrains 50
Beacon 51
Audience 53
A Corpse Turns Cold 54
My Translators 56
Night of the Amnesty 57
Imperial Command 59
Endless Silence 60
Return 61

Orhan Veli Kanık | I Am Listening to Istanbul 62
For You 64
This World 65
Living 66
Exodus 67
For Our Homeland 68
Just for the Hell of It 69

Oktay Rifat | The Flute 70
A Formidable Gypsy 71

Melih Cevdet Anday | On the Nomad Sea 72
Startling Encounter 78
The Flower of Darkness 79
Are We Going To Live Without Aging? 80

	Vertigo *81*
	Copper Age *82*
	The Battle of Kadesh *84*
	From: Odysseus Bound *85*
Behçet Necatigil	Time of Death *87*
	Limit *88*
	Dark Dominion *89*
Cahit Külebi	A Story of the Sea *90*
İlhan Berk	Dead *91*
	For Homer *93*
Ceyhun Atuf Kansu	The Critics *94*
	The Daily Rose *96*
Salâh Birsel	Geography Lesson *97*
Sabahattin Kudret Aksal	Old Night *99*
Necati Cumalı	Mozart's Birds *100*
Özdemir Asaf	Aphorisms *101*
Attilâ İlhan	Ancient Sea Folk *102*
	The Dead Have Grown Old *105*
	Captain *106*
	Another Man *108*
Can Yücel	History Lesson at the Flea Market *111*
Ümit Yaşar Oğuzcan	The Left Ear of the Grand Vizier *114*
Nüzhet Erman	The Big Tale *115*
Turgut Uyar	And Came the Tailors *116*
	Deer Night *120*
Metin Eloğlu	Rasp *123*

Edip Cansever	Vanish 124
	Bedouin 126
	Crab 127
Talat S. Halman	The Desolate Locust 130
Cemal Süreya	Blood Lurks Under All Words 137
	Just at These Hours 139
Ece Ayhan	Monument of the Unknown Student 141
	Kindertotenlieder 142
	The Voice of Poetry by the Seashore 143
Gülten Akın	Rain 144
Ahmet Oktay	All Men Die 145
Kemal Özer	All the King's Men 148
	Like a Flame 149
	The Tuft 150
Hilmi Yavuz	now for whatever reason 151
Özdemir İnce	In Praise of My Father 152
	Our Sons 153
Ferit Edgü	*From: Lecture Notes* 155
Ülkü Tamer	The Dagger 157
	Sunday in the Meadows 158
	Responses for Poetry 159
Turgay Gönenç	Unexpected Sights 162
Cahit Zarifoğlu	Toward Freedom 163
Ataol Behramoğlu	Some Day for Sure 166
Sennur Sezer	To Stay Out of the Fight 169
İsmet Özel	A Shroud for My Darling 170

Enis Batur Lot's Woman *172*

Murathan Mungan Last Swans *173*

Ahmet Erhan Waiting Beside a Friend's Coffin *174*

Biographical Notes *177*
About the Editors *187*
Acknowledgments *189*

Preface

"Four out of three Turks," Aziz Nesin, Turkey's premier satirist, once quipped, "are poets." His fanciful observation was apt to a great extent especially prior to modern times when the poetic arts seemed to be a consuming passion and a popular pastime. Ottoman sultans reveled in verse, and often turned out poems themselves. For the urban intellectuals, versifying was virtually a requisite. In the seventeenth century, Sultan Murad IV sent orders to his commander in chief in meter and rhyme, and the commander replied employing the same meter and rhyme sequence. In the countryside, folk poets provided much-loved entertainment through their lyric songs. With some eminent poets denigrating prose, the supremacy of poetry overshadowed the growth of prose as a vehicle of expression. Poetry was so popular that, even in the latter part of the nineteenth century, compilers of dictionaries felt it necessary to put them in meter and rhyme from beginning to end, e.g., Turkish-French, Turkish-Armenian, Turkish-Greek lexicons. Even a chemistry textbook was written in verse!

With the growth of newspapers and magazines, essays and articles, fiction and dramatic writing over the last hundred and fifty years, Turkish poetry has experienced a partial eclipse. Nevertheless, in comparison with many other nations, it still holds sway. In intellectual circles poetry sometimes emerges as a matter of life and death. Significantly, the most influential Turkish Communist ever was not a statesman or a sociologist or a journalist, but the poet Nazım Hikmet.

Although the novel is gaining ascendancy in contemporary Turkish literature, thanks to the stature of Yaşar Kemal and Orhan Pamuk at home and abroad, fiction in Turkey still shares the limelight with poetry.

Arguably, the place of honor in the history of Turkish literature belongs to poetry. That holds true for nearly twelve centuries from the sixth century A.D. onward. Among Central Asian Turks (particularly the Uighurs) during long migrations into Asia Minor, in the Anatolian Selçuk period (eleventh-thirteenth century), and in the six centuries of the Ottoman Empire (from the end of the thirteenth century to the first quarter of the twentieth), it was principally the poets who gave voice to social, ethical, and aesthetic concerns; represented verbal creativity; constituted the vanguard of new orientations; and served as custodians of established values. Those poets also helped disseminate Chinese, Islamic (within an Arabo-Persian context), and eventually European-American cultural influences.

In the course of this time-honored tradition, Turkish poetry proved amazingly prolific, especially during the Ottoman period. Elite poets, most of whom were close to the royal court and enjoyed patronage, produced a vast corpus of formal verse in stanzaic forms, strict prosodic structure, and stringent rhyme sequences influenced by Arabo-Persian models. Troubadours and itinerant bards of the rural areas perpetuated the indigenous hallmarks of Turkic/Turkish folk poetry, much of it improvised and sung to musical accompaniment, using syllabic meters, lilting rhythms, and an authentically Anatolian vocabulary. In both mainstreams, sonority and lyric flow, with frequent alliteration and onomatopoeic effects, played a major role. In a significant sense, both classical and folk poetry possessed a musical quality.

Cultural modernization brought in its wake and was, to a certain extent, pioneered by innovations and revolutionary ideas introduced in the works of twentieth-century poets. The transformation of Turkish poetry has been astounding in the varieties of the influences it received from the West, not the least being the enthusiastic use of organic form and free verse—and in the way it evolved a character of its own that can be described as "truly original." Following decades of soul-searching as well as a feverish search for fresh modes of expression, a brave new synthesis seems to be emerging. Interestingly, modern verse, in its diverse leanings, has embraced such European movements as Parnassianism, symbolism, surrealism, constructivism, and others along with its own authentic traditions of *poesia d'arte* and *poesia popolare.*

Since the establishment of the Turkish Republic in 1923, the typology of Turkish verse has possessed an astonishingly broad range, from Sufism to social(ist) realism, from romantic love to ideological invective, from metaphysical concerns to *léttrisme,* from didactic verse to historical nostalgia, from neoclassical reformulations to futuristic probes.

The one hundred poems in this volume have been selected with some basic regard for their representativeness although no attempt has been made to be all-inclusive in terms of typology. For example, the selection does not include any chauvinistic or patently ideological poems. By the same token, it excludes didactic verse and outright propaganda.

The volume may be considered truly representative in the sense that no major poet who gained stature since the 1920s has been omitted—although it has proven impossible to do justice to the several hundred poets active in a period longer than eight decades. It would be foolhardy to claim that the poems here are definitely the best poems of the poets who appear in the anthology. One can assert with confidence, however, that many important poems published since the 1920s are included. In the last analysis, all we can do is to offer apologies to poets and regrets for poems not incorporated into *A Brave New Quest.* It should be noted, under any circumstances, that the reasons for some exclusions are related to untranslatability—or, at least, to the possibility of excessive loss in the transpositions.

A Brave New Quest does not intend to serve as a survey or critical study of modern Turkish poetry with its diverse movements. It is merely a coterie of some of the best work by Turkish poets, arranged not thematically nor grouped in terms of movements, but in chronological order of the poets' years of birth from 1901 to 1958. This volume is presented for the purpose of poetic enjoyment. The poems speak for themselves.

The translator would like to assure the readers that he has taken care to convey the spirit, structure, and style of the originals in the English versions. He hopes that the poems here will provide some pleasure while collectively furnishing a sense of the lyrics and dynamics of modern Turkey.

Talat S. Halman

Note on Turkish Spelling

For modern Turkish authors, place names, publications, and special terms, this volume employs standard Turkish spelling. The biographical notes are arranged according to the modern Turkish alphabet that appears below.

a (like *gun*); var. â (like *are*)
b (as in English)
c (like *jade*)
ç (*ch* of *chin*)
d (as in English)
e (like *pen*)
f (as in English)
g (*g* of *good*)
ğ (makes preceding vowel longer)
h (*h* of *half*)
ı (like second vowel of *portable*)
i (like *it*); var. î (like *eat*)
j (like *measure*)
k (*k* of *king*)
l (as in English)
m (as in English)
n (as in English)
o (like *eau* in French)
ö (like *bird* or French *deux*)
p (as in English)
r (*r* of *rust*)
s (*s* of *sun*)
ş (*sh* of *shine*)
t (as in English)
u (like *pull*); var. û (like *pool*)
ü (like *tu* in French)
v (as in English)
y (*y* of *you*)
z (as in English)

Exceptions include words which have become common in English and appear in English dictionaries in anglicized forms. Proper names have been kept in modern Turkish with two major exceptions— İstanbul and İzmir have been rendered with normal English spelling using *I* rather than *İ*.

Poems

Fear

I have the fear of all the things that end,
I am the Blue Eagle who drags the dawn
Along in his iron beak . . .
                                        And life is caught
Within my claws like dangling emeralds
And deathlessness along my lovely swoop
Now bites the thirsty antelope of time.

Ahmet Hamdi Tanpınar

Awakening

And now life's desolate twilight hour starts
Beyond distant cypresses daylight departs.

The gardens of spring don the brightest sun,
The river's voice rises and then is gone.

The nightingale sings of love's sorrows
While rings of fire burn the rims of the rose.

Ahmet Hamdi Tanpınar

Today Is Sunday

Today is Sunday.
For the first time they took me out into the sun today
And for the first time in my life I was aghast
that the sky is so far away
                and so blue
                and so vast
                        I stood there without motion.
Then I sat on the ground in respectful devotion
leaning against the white wall.
Who cares about the waves with which I yearn to roll
Or about strife or freedom or my wife right now.
The soil, the sun, and me . . .
I feel so happy.

Nazım Hikmet

Silence

Outside,
in the air whose flintlocks have their sparks flying,
looms a brigand in black breeches with flashing stripes.

Outside,
twenty profligates from the Askeroz valley
are doing their wild dance.

Outside . . .

Yet, we keep quiet inside.
No arrow cast from the wing of a black eagle
is lodged in the neck of our silence.

Outside . . .

Yet, inside we keep quiet:
Our silence doesn't wear an old frock coat
whose buttons are fastened.

Outside,
the smell of saffron
    floats in the wind like ships of fire.

Outside . . .

Yet, inside we keep quiet,
the way a bullet keeps quiet in its cartridge.
If there is an echo in the dome of the sky
louder than our silence, let it cry out!

Outside,
In the dark,
the sea is bursting open like a forest struck in its groin.

Inside, we keep quiet,
and the dungeon is silent
    like a wounded animal
        whose blood is trickling into its heart.

Nazım Hikmet

From: The Epic of the War of Liberation

THEY

They are teeming like ants in the ground
                                        fish in the sea
                                          birds in the air,
they are timid
            brave
              ignorant
                  wise
                      or childish,
and they are the ones who destroy
             and create:
in our epic there are only their adventures.

They who are led astray by the traitor's ploy
             and drop their flags on the ground
they who leave the battlefield to the enemy
             and run away to hide at home
they who draw their daggers on all those renegades
and who laugh like a green tree
and weep untimely tears
and even swear at mother and wife,
in our epic there are only their adventures.

The destiny
          of iron
               coal
                 sugar
and red copper
and textiles
and all branches of industry

and love
            and tyranny
                        and life
and the sky
            and the wilderness
                        and the blue ocean
and riverbeds full of sorrow
plowed land and big cities
            that fate will suddenly change one day at dawn,
at the edge of darkness at daybreak
            when they straighten up by pressing on the earth
                     with their heavy and calloused hands.

They are the ones
who reflect the brightest forms on the wisest mirrors.
In our century they triumphed
                     and they were defeated.
So much has been said about them.
It was said about them that
"They have nothing to lose but their chains."

Nazım Hikmet

From: The Epic of Sheikh Bedreddin[1]

It was hot,
so hot.
The heat
        was a dull dagger with a blood-drenched handle.

It was hot.
The clouds were loaded,
they were about to burst
                ready to burst.
Without making a move, he looked:
        his eyes, like two eagles, swooped
                down from the rocks
                into the plain.
There, the softest and hardest,
the thriftiest and most generous,
the most
            loving,
the grandest and loveliest woman:
                        the EARTH
                    was about
                        to give birth.

It was hot.
From the Karaburun[2] mountains, he gazed,
                with knitted eyebrows,
at the horizon at the end of this earth.
Plucking children's heads like bloody poppies
                in the meadows

1. *The Epic of Sheikh Bedreddin,* published in 1936, might well be Nazım Hikmet's masterpiece. A moving account of the rise and fall of a heretical sect that preached an incipient form of communism in the early fifteenth century, it contains some of the most poignant poetic narrative passages ever written in the Turkish language.

2. Karaburun: A mountainous region in western Turkey.

and dragging stark-naked screams in its wake,
a five-crested fire burst forth from the horizon
                                        that it engulfed.

This was
                the Royal Heir Murad[3]
to whom the Sultan had issued an edict
that he hasten to the province of Aydın[4]
and crush Bedreddin's deputy Mustafa the heretic.

It was hot.
Bedreddin's deputy Mustafa the heretic looked.
Peasant Mustafa looked
                he looked without fear
                      without anger or a smile.
He looked
                straight ahead
                      without wavering.
The softest and hardest,
the thriftiest and most generous,
the most
                loving, the grandest and loveliest woman:
                                                                the EARTH
                                                          was about
                                                                to give birth.

He looked.
Bedreddin's comrades looked from the rocks to the horizon:
The end of the earth kept coming closer
          on the wings of a bird of death carrying a royal edict.
And yet those brave men
          who were looking from the rocks

3. Murad: The royal prince who later became Sultan Murad I.

4. Aydın: A province in western Turkey.

had opened up this land
with its grapes and figs and pomegranates
and its sheep with fleece blonder than honey
        milk thicker than honey,
with its narrow-rumped, lion-maned horses.
Like a table for brothers they had opened up this land
        without walls or boundaries.

It was hot.
He looked.
Bedreddin's comrades looked at the horizon . . .
The softest and hardest,
the thriftiest and most generous,
the most
            loving,
the grandest and loveliest woman:
                        the EARTH
                    was about
                        to give birth.

It was hot.
The clouds were loaded.
The first drop, like a sweet word, was about to fall.
Suddenly,
            as if pouring from the rocks
                    raining down from the sky
                        sprouting out of the soil
like the ultimate creation of this earth,
Bedreddin's warriors confronted the Royal Heir's army.
They were wearing seamless white robes,
                    their heads were bare
                        feet bare, swords bare.

It was a ruthless battle.

Turkish peasants from Aydın
Greek sailors from Chios[5]
Jewish artisans
Börklüce Mustafa's ten thousand heretical comrades
tore into the forest of enemies like ten thousand axes.
The ranks with red and green banners,
emblazoned shields and bronze helmets
were shattered to pieces
but as the day sank into evening in the torrential rain
the ten thousand were but two thousand.

To sing their songs in unison,
to drag the nets together out of the water,
to work the iron together like lace
to be able to plow the land together
and to eat the honey-filled figs together
to be able to say
"Together in everything
together everywhere
except the lover's face"
the ten thousand gave their eight thousand . . .
They were defeated.

The victors wiped the blood off their swords
on the seamless white robes
of the vanquished.
And the earth they had tilled together, with their brotherly hands
like a song sung together
was trampled
under the hooves of horses bred in the Edirne[6] Palace.

* * *

5. Chios: An Aegean island (now belonging to Greece) called Sakız in Turkish.
6. Edirne: Adrianopolis, the Ottoman capital of the time.

It's drizzling,
fearful,
whispering
like the talk of treason.

Drizzling,
like the patter of the white bare feet of renegades
on damp dark earth.

Drizzling.
In the marketplace of Serez,[7]
across from a coppersmith's shop,
my Bedreddin is hanging from a tree.

Drizzling.
Late on a starless night,
and getting soaked in the rain
swinging from a leafless branch
    is the stark-naked body of my sheikh.

Drizzling.
The market of Serez is mute,
the market of Serez is blind.
In the air hovers the accursed sorrow of not speaking, not seeing
And the market of Serez has covered its face with its hand.
It's drizzling.

Nazım Hikmet

7. Serez: A small town in present-day Greece.

Quatrains

I

"Fill your cup with wine before it is filled with dust," Khayyam said.
A man with a long snout and tattered shoes went by Khayyam's rose-bed
Saying: "Abundance in this world numbers more than all the stars, yet I go hungry:
"How can I buy wine when I can't even afford to buy bread?"

II

Bittersweet thoughts of death, of how short life is,
sipping wine in a tulip-garden under the moon . . .
Since our birth in the basement of a pitch-dark house in the slums
such sweet melancholy thoughts have never been our good fortune.

III

Life is slipping by, seize the day before you sink into inexorable sleep;
pour ruby wine into your crystal cup. It's daybreak, lad, your sleep is so deep.
Wake up. So, in his ice-cold room without curtains the youth gets up:
it just doesn't forgive tardiness, the factory whistle with that nagging beep.

IV

I never feel nostalgic about bygone days
—except for one summer day I miss—
even the dying gleam of my blue eyes
will bear you tidings of the coming day of bliss.

V

I am a man: I, Nazım Hikmet
the Turkish poet,
full of faith tip to toe
full of struggle, yearning, and hope for the best days yet.

VI

A newscaster, I read
with a voice heavy and naked like a seed:
"Here now is my heart's correct time:
        at the crack of dawn the gong will be heard."

Nazım Hikmet

About Living

I

Living is not a joking matter:
you have to live with great seriousness
like a squirrel, for instance,
that is to say, without expecting anything outside or beyond living,
which means, you must devote yourself fully to living.

You have to take living seriously,
in such a way, to such an extent
that, for instance, your hands tied behind you, your back to the wall,
or wearing thick spectacles and a white robe,
in a laboratory,
you must be willing to die for other people,
even those whose faces you have never seen,
although nobody has forced you to do this
and although you know that living
is the most beautiful and the most genuine thing.

That is to say, you have to take living so seriously
that, for instance, even at age seventy, you will plant olive trees
and not to leave them to your children, either,
but because you don't believe in death although you fear it,
because, I mean, living carries greater weight.

II

Say we're gravely ill, must have surgery,
that is to say
there's a strong chance we'll never get up from the white table.
Although it's impossible not to feel sad about leaving a little prematurely,
nonetheless we'll laugh at the irreverent jokes people tell,
and we'll look out the window to see if it's a rainy day,
or wait impatiently for the latest news on the radio.

Say, for the sake of things worth fighting for,
say, we're at the battlefront
where, during the first offensive on the first day,
it is possible to fall face down and die.
We'll be aware of this with a strange fury,
but we'll still wonder like mad
about the outcome of the war which is to last many years.

Say we're in prison,
age almost fifty
with eighteen years to go before the iron doors will open.

And yet we're going to live together with the outside world,
with its people, animals, struggles, and winds,
that is to say the world beyond the walls,
which means, no matter how we are or where we are
life must be lived as if there'll be no dying . . .

III

This globe will grow cold,
a star among stars,
and one of the tiniest,
that is to say, a speck of gilt on blue velvet:
that's what our immense world is.

Some day, this globe will grow cold,
it will tumble and float
not even like a heap of ice
or a dead cloud,
but like a walnut shell
in the jet-black darkness of endless space.

You'll have to bear the grief of this even now,
its sadness you must already feel.
This is the way this world must be loved
        if you're going to be able to say: "I have lived."

Nazım Hikmet

[untitled]

Let us give the world to the children at least for one day
Let them play with it as if it's a spangled balloon
Let them sing and dance among the stars

Let us give the world to the children
Like a huge apple or a warm loaf of bread
        at least for one day
        so that they'll have enough to eat

Let us give the world to the children
        so that even if it's for one day
        it will learn what friendship is

The children will take the world
        out of our hands
        and they will plant immortal trees

Nazım Hikmet

No Tree Has Ever Given Such Marvelous Fruit

The most perfect offspring
          of earth fire and sea
shall be born of us . . .

      And people
            without a fear
            without a thought
will trust their hands to each other
and looking at the stars together
                    they will say:
"Living is so wonderful!"
Deep as human eyes
      cool like a bunch of grapes
                              soothing
                                   comforting
they will sing
               an unheard-of song
No tree
will have given
               such marvelous fruit.

And even the most promising
          midsummer night
                will never have arrived at dawn
                    with such melodies
                    in such incredible colors.

The most perfect offspring
          of earth
                fire
                    and sea
shall be born of us . . .

Nazım Hikmet

Anguish

ALLEGRO

There descended a voice from the realms lost:
"This man shall drag the void along his nape!"
Suddenly the roof overhead was tossed
The day a crack left the heavens agape.

All hell broke loose, I saw from my window;
It came true, the old witches' augury:
Eternal life a gauze on his arrow,
The hunter of the skies took aim at me.

It burnt my life's gem at once to ashes
When I felt the arrow's flaming venom;
Grappling with death as in headlong crashes,
My inmost mouth spewed out my cranium.

Like a tiny teapot, the world convulsed,
Bearings burned out as the void went astray,
Fact and fantasy alike were repulsed,
Both wisdom and folly in disarray.

A sledge beat on the anvil of my head;
Into my bed, my last resort, I curled.
A speckled hen, as the aurora bled,
Made a gift to me of a brave new world.

This is an odd world that baffles the sage
Where place is surface and time illusion.
The universe builds us a fleeting stage
Where mankind is duped into delusion.

What are you? Even if you're real, go away.
Hurry, blindness; rush, false eye, come over.
Let your shapes settle in my soul and stay,
My land and master, my friend and lover.

ADAGIO

Month after month I roamed broken, aghast:
My soul was a cauldron that my mind drained;
With the madmen's town one horizon past,
My brain's fantasies were bridled and chained.

Why do all things in the distance dwindle?
In eyeless dreams who gives me piercing sight?
Why the dance of time in the globe's spindle?
I crave wisdom to see my life's twilight.

Thoughts burn as vitriol in the wound's grail
Clinging like leeches to the brain's membranes.
Hail, most majestic of agonies, hail,
Magic log that blooms as it sears and pains.

Guide me, I implore, where my riddle gapes;
Layers of heaven, tear down your mystery.
Mothers' prayers, fall and turn into drapes;
Carve out a scepter for me, ancient tree.

Even to killers sleep offers its rest
And quilts cover up the godless and all.
Others suck nectar from its soothing breast
But comfort's spring hands me a sand-filled bowl.

Is it the madness of dreams that I sipped—
A shrapnel burst in search of its secret?
Seized by spasms on the vines, a satyr's lust gripped
A plucked skull with the ants' palace in it.

Cell by cell, a scorpion stung my brain;
I ran from season to season. I know
Neither the stake nor the rack gives more pain
Than the savage torture of the mind's woe.

ANDANTE

My soul weaves a knot that no one can break:
Why this fear of death, why the tears I shed?
Frightened, under fathomless skies I shake,
What is there in distances that I dread?

Horizons drift, sly as a fox in flight;
Roads coil and recoil like entangled seams.
The wizard who conjures my dreams each night
Now lures me with the blue light that he beams.

Why vent your vengeance on me, sorceress?
What black fume is that raging in your lair?
Into my poisoned, bleeding brain you press
A deathly sword sharp as glass, thin as hair.

Dictionaries, find a word for my plight!
A name that all men can identify.
You, my ragged garments, hold my hand tight.
You, mirrors, divulge to me: Who am I?

Or, tell me, am I perhaps one of those
Mythic heifers on whose horns stands the earth,
A plot earmarked by the builder of woes,
Banished from life, condemned to pain and death?

I falter like a soft tender butterfly
That carries the mountains on its frail wings,
A speck of dust pregnant to the whole sky
From which my gargantuan anguish springs.

Neither lies can devise nor truth conjure
The design I see with closed eyes only.
I searched in vain: There is not in nature
So much ascent and descent as in me.

FINALE

In the dead of night suddenly I fall
Into the dark ditch of life's true nature
And solve the most baffling riddle of all
The riddle of time past and time future.

Open, sesame, open! The gates swung:
An atlas couch, our heavenly father,
Crystal palace where bright chandeliers hung,
Sacred edifice of endless matter.

Atoms had a carnival, wined and dined,
And rays of light danced and pranced all around.
Forms were intricate and life intertwined
I saw God, who is unknown though renowned.

The world bulged as the ocean at flood tide,
Swelling and rising, nearly drowning me.
A glitter on the water where all paths hide,
And the sense of eternal life at sea.

Come, union and harmony, redeem me:
I can no longer play the phantom's part;
Hand over verse-making to the pigmy,
I now set my sights on the supreme art.

To soar beyond is my burning desire,
Distance is my crop and time my gold mine;
It's to the Milky Way that I aspire,
And the pearls of fathomless lakes are mine.

Kneel before me, Fate, and forsake your might;
My bag bulges with causes rolled into one;
You are the root where all branches unite.
I crave everlasting life from now on.

Necip Fazıl Kısakürek

Abraham

abraham
knock down the idols in me
with the axe in your hand
who's propping up new idols
to replace the broken ones

the sun smashed my house of ice
huge blocks of ice came crashing down
breaking the necks of the idols
abraham
who took the sun into my house

nebuchadnezzar turned into idols
the lovely women strolling the hanging gardens
having embraced the timeless gardens
I have kept those women to myself

abraham
who is it that takes my heart for an idol and breaks it

Asaf Halet Çelebi

Two Solitary Trees

Two trees by an odd creek that flows alone
        Stand young strong full-grown;
They have something to say, they do, and yet,
        Dead or alive, they always keep quiet.

After sunset, under the stars, see the way
        The trees sway,
Whatever they have to hold back or declare,
        Dead or alive, it is all laid bare.

By the creek two desolate trees stand
        Pegged onto the ground;
They have something to say, they do, and yet,
        Dead or alive, they have said it—or not.

Ahmet Muhip Dıranas

Poem at Thirty-Five

Age thirty-five: that means half the course,
Like Dante, we stand midway in life;
All our youthful vigor and resource
—Wanton is our plea, in vain our strife—
Drift away blind to tears of remorse . . .

Look at my temples, are they snow-clad?
O my God, is this wrinkled face me?
These eyes rimmed with rings purple and sad?
Why are you now my arch enemy,
Mirrors, the best friends I ever had?

All this change is more than I can bear:
None of my pictures here could be mine.
Where did all those days of joy go, where?
Can't be me, this man smiling, benign.
It's a lie that I am free of care.

Our first love looks hazy, far away,
A memory driven from the heart.
Friends who set out with us on life's way
Took separate paths and strayed apart.
Now our loneliness grows day by day.

Odd, I now find that the sky can turn
Into other hues, that stone is hard,
That the waters drown and the flames burn,
And each new day brings a painful load—
All these at thirty-five I could learn.

Autumn, quince yellow, pomegranate red;
Each year I feel it's closer to me.
Why do these birds circle overhead?
And these ravaged gardens that I see?
What funeral is this? Who is dead?

Immutably death is all men's fate.
"Slept, never woke," will be the story,
And who knows where or why or how late?
You shall have but one prayer's glory
On your stone-bier throne lying in state.

Cahit Sıtkı Tarancı

After Death

With many hopes about death we perished,
But the charm was broken in a vacuum.
Our song of love we cannot help exhume,
A view of the sky, tuft of twigs, bird's plume;
Living was a habit we had cherished.

No news comes from the world now or ever;
No one misses us, no soul cares to know,
The darkness of our night is endless, so
We might just as well do without a window:
Our image has faded from the river.

Cahit Sıtkı Tarancı

Terror

Gently daylight recoiled from the windowpane
Baring all the mirrors desolate and stark;
Now in the gardens the voices of silence reign
And the dome of the sky is a blotch of dark.

From fountains and springs water has ceased to pour
So our empty glasses may be filled no more;
Where narcissus had bloomed, now a Minotaur
Forbids passage to the birds that flee in vain.

Scylla is precious and so is Charybdis.
I fear the night and its dark-ridden abyss:
My trusted hills may suddenly go amiss
And beyond them dawn may never break again.

Cahit Sıtkı Tarancı

The Saga of Istanbul

Say Istanbul and a seagull comes to mind
Half-silver and half-foam, half-fish and half-bird.
Say Istanbul and a fable comes to mind,
The old wives' tale that we have all heard.

Say Istanbul and a mighty steamship comes to mind
Whose songs are sung in the adobe huts of Anatolia;
Milk flows out of her taps, roses bloom on her masts;
My childhood in Anatolia's adobe huts
Sail to Istanbul and back on that mighty steamship.

Say Istanbul and mottled grapes come to mind
With three candles burning bright on the basket—
Suddenly along comes a girl so ruthlessly female,
With a figure so lovely that I'd give up my life for it,
Her lips ripe with grape honey,
A girl luscious and lustful from tip to toe—
Southern wind and willow branch and the dance of joy—
Hailing from a wine cellar, she makes you tipsy;
As the song goes, "Like a ship at sea
My heart is tossed and wrecked again."

Say Istanbul and the Grand Bazaar comes to mind:
Beethoven's Ninth hand in hand with the Algerian March;
And an immaculate bridal bedroom set
Is auctioned off without the bride and the groom.
A chubby lute inlaid with mother-of-pearl
Recalls the famous lutanist on old records.
Brandishing candlesticks and hookahs and rusty Persian swords.
American cowboys pop up:
"Hands up!"

American sailors wear lily-white uniforms
Plucked from a huge daisy, pure as milk, clean as a cloud;

Death looks ugly on so pure a white,
But when they fight
They put their combat uniforms on
—Color of blood and gunpowder and smoke—
Which gather hate but no dirt.

Say Istanbul and a huge fishery comes to mind
Like a rusty cobweb over the Bosphorus,
Or sprawling off the Marmara coast.
Forty tunnies toss in the fishery like forty millstones.
The tunny, after all, is the king of the sea:
You must shoot it in the eye with a rifle and fell it like a tree,
Then suddenly the face of the fishery gets bloodshot
And the emerald waters become muddled in the turmoil.
With forty tunnies at a clip, the skipper is spellbound for joy.
A seagull perched on the mast catches a mackerel in midair
and gobbles it,
Then it flies away without waiting for one more;
The fisherman smiles, sweet and kind:
"That gull's Maria," he says,
"That's the way she comes and goes, always."

Say Istanbul and the Prince Island [1] comes to mind
Where the French language is murdered
By sixtyish matrons who sit around puffed up as hell;
If only the lonely pine trees there could tell
All about the dalliance of the boy with the gal.

Say Istanbul and towers come to mind:
If I do a painting of one, the other one grumbles.

1. Prince Island (Büyükada): The largest of the islands in an archipelago of nine, near Istanbul.

The Maiden's Tower[2] ought to know that's the way the cookie crumbles:
She should marry the Galata Tower[3] and have lots of kids.

Say Istanbul and a waterfront street comes to mind:
Anatolia's poor godforsaken huddled masses land
In its coffeehouses day after day,
Some must go begging to survive, but shame keeps them away;
A few manage to find a broom and become street cleaners—no less,
Their faces smeared with a filthy fusty grin;
Others shoulder a pannier or an ornate backsaddle,
And they all get lost in the city's hubbub and commotion.
Tied to a greasy girth, some carry a piano on their backs
Their legs wobbly under the weight, melting like wax,
They pant and heave, drenched in sweat.
A gentle porter is a must for a fragile item.
Do the tender hands value a piano the way the porter does?
Suddenly a mushy voice blares on the radio across the street:
The most popular crooner of them all,
Yelping and yawning, smudged with the greasy perfumes of Arabia:
"Life is full of joy and sorrow,
"Some stay and some go."

Say Istanbul and a stadium comes to mind
Where twenty-five thousand voices under the sun
Sing our national anthem in unison
And the clouds are fired like cannonballs.
Dazzled by the sight of twenty-five thousand strong
I rejoice in their joyful song
And offer to pluck my heart for them like a red poppy.

2. Maiden's Tower: A tiny tower on a pinpoint island at the entrance to Istanbul's harbor.

3. Galata Tower: Tower in a district of the same name on Istanbul's European side. It was built by the Genoese in 1348.

Say Istanbul and a stadium comes to mind
Where my blood flows into the veins of my fellow men.
Rubbing shoulders, we holler together
Till our throats are sore:
Lefter's[4] kick is a sure score.

Say Istanbul and a stadium comes to mind
Where multitudes share the grandeur of the joy
Born at the same moment:
Myriads and millions
Band together in my head.
Then a line out of a poem fearfully flutters in the air:
"Blessed are those who embrace their loved ones."

Say Istanbul and Yahya Kemal[5] used to come to mind;
Nowadays it's Orhan Veli[6] whose name is on the tip of my tongue;
His flair and flamboyance, his poems and his face
Hover overhead like a wounded pigeon
Which descends quietly to perch on this poem.
Where?
Just look, you'll find it there.

This city just drives you out of your mind;
Good thing Orhan Veli's drinking glasses remain behind.

Say Istanbul and Sait Faik[7] comes to mind:
Pebbles twitter on the shore of Burgaz Island,[8]

4. Lefter: A very famous soccer player.

5. Yahya Kemal (Beyatlı): A famous neoclassical poet (1884–1958) who wrote many poems in praise of Istanbul.

6. Orhan Veli (Kanık): A poet famous for numerous poems about Istanbul; he died in 1950 at the age of thirty-six.

7. Sait Faik (Abasıyanık): A leading short-story writer, who lived from 1906 to 1954.

8. Burgaz Island: One of the larger islands in the archipelago near Istanbul. Sait Faik's principal residence, now the Sait Faik Museum, is located on this island.

While a blue-eyed boy grows up in circles of joy
A blue-eyed old fisherman grows younger and tinier,
When they reach the same height they turn into Sait
And they roam the city hand in hand,
Cursing beast and bird, friend and foe alike!
On Sivriada[9] they gather gulls' eggs,
By midnight they're in the red-light district,
In the morning they go through Galata:[10]
At the café they kid around with a harmless lunatic,
"Whaddya know," they say. "You're holding the paper upside down."
Then they set the poor guy's newspaper on fire,
Then they sit and weep quietly.

Say Istanbul and Sait Faik comes to mind
All over this town's rock and soil and water,
A friend of the poor and the sick,
Whose pencil is as sharp as his heart is wounded,
Bleeding for the lonely and yearning for the pure and the good.

Say Istanbul and Sait's last years come to mind:
At his best age he's told he has just a few years to live;
How could Sait bear the thought of it?
The blue-eyed boy doesn't give a damn,
But the old fisherman broods like hell;
And a green venom bursts out of the sea
Piercing the heart that feels, ravaging the mind that knows.

The little blue-eyed boy
And the old fisherman
And that green venom smeared all over our lips . . .
So long as Istanbul throbs alive in the sea,
So long as language lives, so will Sait's poetry.

9. Sivriada: An uninhabited island in the archipelago near Istanbul.
10. Galata: A district in the city of Istanbul.

Say Istanbul and a gypsy woman comes to mind
With a bunch of flowers taller than herself,
Wherever the spring comes from, so does she.
No crackpot that woman, but every inch a gypsy,
She is the sun and the soil from tip to toe,
And a mother matchless among mothers:
One kid on her back, one at her breast, one in her tummy.
A gypsy woman always bulges with a baby.
Devil may care, her life has flair:
She roams the city from one end to the other
Humbly selling tongs or doing the belly dance.
"How about a quarter, dear?" she says,
"You want me to tell your fortune, love?"
Till the day she dies, she tells nothing but lies.
Then comes the dream she had the night before:
"I see a yellow snake. Son-of-a-bitch keeps bugging me.
I wake up and what do I see?
My little ones are on the edge of the bed sucking my toes."

Say Istanbul and a textile factory comes to mind:
High walls, long counters, tall stoves . . .
Tender slender girls toil all day long on their feet,
In blood and sweat, weary and sad,
Their faces long their hands long their days long
In the factory where the windows are near the ceiling.
Red-heeled fair-skinned girls—"No loitering, girls!"

Rows and rows of trees stretch out there,
But the endless walls cut the girls off from them,
From the amber fields and the purple streets
Where the fair season rumbles and tumbles.
A nineteen-year-old working mother,
Is dazzled by the white foamy flow of silk
Which whets her appetite no end, she gets ideas;
But printed silk is no good to make pants for her sons.
Now if she could get a bolt of ivory-white calico:

She can do much with it: drapes and sheets and underwear;
The very thought of ivory-white calico dazzles her.
When she dies giving birth to a third son,
She still longs for a bolt of calico.
Young mothers like her are a dime a dozen:
At the factory somebody else takes the place of this one.
That's the way it is: If one goes, another comes.
Damn you death.

Say Istanbul and a barge comes to mind
Brimful of onions, green as poison on coral red,
Sailing in from the Black Sea ports winter and summer
With one more patch on its filthy sail each time
And the rust of its iron rods on our tongues
And its motors speeding along our pulsebeats right into our hearts.
A mermaid with huge scale-covered buttocks.

Say Istanbul and a barge comes to mind
Demure and heedless
Called the *Sea Tiger* or the *Triumphant Sword.*

Say Istanbul and Sinan the great architect[11] comes to mind
His ten fingers soaring like ten mighty plane trees.
Then the monster of the shacks and shanties rears its head
Where smoke and filth and blight ruthlessly spread.
With giant's breasts our city suckles dwarfs.

Bedri Rahmi Eyuboğlu

11. Sinan (1489–1588): Chief architect of the Ottoman Empire for five decades.

From: The Epic of Çakır

—Clarity, in the form of hands and feet, made him uneasy.

I decided I shall die
In the midst of mighty rivers, without fear.
In the light and with remote inscriptions,
The fact will hang and stay around my neck
Like an amulet with a prayer.

Years ago, before the blue age of the seeds,
I decided, with the consent of the birds of night,
I shall surround myself with big empty beakers,
And with the thirst of dried-up corpses,
Like a sultan I shall stare at them in delight.

Lighter than air, more ancient than some women,
The truth of our stark-naked birth . . .
Perpetual in cities and hills the world over
Time's beauty sways with the flora,
A remembrance cherished for its worth.

Slowly, like rocks and logs
Within the mind's adultery,
From the white and bright sky of history,
I decided I shall die
And share with animal skeletons life's mystery.

Fazıl Hüsnü Dağlarca

In Passage

Beneath the giant stars our world is tiny
And our home a miniature.
Wild flowers cast their spell before dawn
Without memories or sleep.
Mint is their lure.

Everyone is in a trance since bygone days.
All things, in a way, are in rapture.
The coy mistress is divined in the girding space.
In the air the birds glide with love,
And the skies change in grandeur.

The heart observes nothing.
Its madness is pure.
Through our body and soul
Time passes
With its total torture!

Fazıl Hüsnü Dağlarca

Ugly

It's ugly, darling, your lips' scarlet blotch
Against bloodless nature.
While this land sleeps, and the globe far away,
As one membrane sleeps in a throng,
It tastes sour.

It's ugly, this trading—
Twenty percent, thirty percent.
The joy of the moments fleets inward.
As memories and loves soar over the bazaars,
We are reborn, alive, unspent.

Meadows crawl, aged and aimless.
Beauty aloft turns ugly, banned
From life's measures, new and tall,
And all we touch fills one palm
Of one hand.

Molded into gardens and figures,
Our school is ugly.
Comfort's endless forest and virtue's mighty sprawl
On the hills, in the streets,
No longer restlessly.

Lies lead him to the essences of truth,
And deceit to the wisdom of the dead:
The shyster in court is ugly.
Crippled more than the blind and the lame,
The infamous pleasure of darkness descends smugly.

Against the valiant times that endure,
Ugly is the midnight.
Skulking in aching bones along distances,
Lie stars, constellations, the whole firmament,
Grand not by mercy, but by inspiring fright.

As it grips the generations of vice and waste
Slowly
Over the disfigured faces of crones,
And as the prayers of young brides go unanswered,
Warfare in history is ugly.

Bugs emit the whirs of the battle for bread.
Trees whine and machines die a slow death.
The hateful geometry of the flesh is clad in dreams.
Though the planets share the same civilization,
The fed and the hungry alike cast an ugly breath.

How could our patience and idiocy
Sleep and not stir in the abyss?
Solace is grim; birds and flowers are futile.
On this bastard earth
How ugly our petty bliss.

As dwarfish as man, as fleeting as life,
What is beauty where the hideous stands grand?
It's ugly, our pain which no grail can contain.
Destiny's ugly from gloom to fearful gloom,
Living dark and degenerate in its homeland.

Death is an unrequited smile, an inevitable affair;
For death's sake we tread on legend's purity.
Ugly are my ancestors of a millennium ago.
Each stone they placed, each fable they believed in
Is dirty.

God lurks numb, and funerals march numb.
In heaven, the shameful deafness of our city—
With the burials the idiot's songs end.
In the buoyancy of love, air, and soil, my friend,
It's ugly: my gravity, your gravity, his gravity.

Fazıl Hüsnü Dağlarca

From: The Epic of the Conquest of Istanbul

EPIC PROLOGUE

Now the darkness of time, like the night,
Passes where no shadows roam.
There, the shores that breathe with God
And Byzantium torn apart from Rome.
Spring is the burden
That the monks with dangling beards must bear
Huge and heavy with rocks and grudge,
On the crenellated banks flanking nowhere.

> Ancient Istanbul, as old as the soul,
> Defies man's age and recall.

A void that spreads along the flavor of the lakes,
Our time has plunged into all or nothing.
Over seven unknowns
The seven hills fling.
The Golden Horn of the world's ox makes no move,
But the water, hemmed in, flurries.
The sleep of the sleepless
Passes bright into the bulk of the centuries.

> Ancient Istanbul, beyond the reach of memory,
> Should be savored gently, without hurry.

The moments of Darius and Sardanapalus
Have come to ruin.
By ships and caravans, teeming, stark-naked,
Those who lost and found love have poured in.
Asian generations stopped at her gates, age by age.

Adoring the eyes of the antelope.
The Prophet's armies sought her warm dreams
With resounding outcries of hope.

> Ancient Istanbul, truly old,
> Where history remains untold.

Hear the tunes of the faithful condemned to be crucified.
Maybe you are the music or the cross.
Which death is real,
Remains your private loss.
East or West cannot be told apart.
The mind heralds the funeral whose images abound.
Your feet, your feet
Are swept off the ground.

> Ancient Istanbul, a voice
> Both remote and close.

Body and soul, yearning, in the pangs of thirst,
Past the time that all the beauties spanned . . .
Sultan Mehmed, the Ottoman Emperor,
One day at dawn marched his galleons overland.
He placed his cannons row by row, in love,
Facing fancy on each side.
In the evening sun, like a tulip,
The brave janissary died.

> Ancient Istanbul, city of the past,
> Whose winds reach God with each gust.

A fog that cloaks the gardens, faces, and the world,
Tongues and creeds came closer in those days.
Out of dungeons, restored to life and light,
Handwritten books rejoice in dreams and rays.
Toward the skies of God, alone and solitary,

Turkish crescents marched on and on.
With the raiders and the volunteers for death
Here the love of the world has begun.

Ancient Istanbul, serene and bygone,
Where life frantically dashes on.

Fazıl Hüsnü Dağlarca

Stone Inscription

The midnight beauty of the trees
Should stop a while.
Flowing waters and far-flung roads
Should stop.

Light in the windows should stop,
Stop for me soon,
Where the day grows with bought-and-sold
The market should stop.

Grass should stop in its silence
When insects quench the soil's hunger.
On desolate mountaintops
The sky should stop its dainty blue.

Mighty birds in the air,
Like huge horses in a ceaseless race—
They should
All stop.

The forest's rampant rustle,
The dream of the fish oceanwide,
Our sleep
Should stop.

Not the dizzy spell of the naked dancers,
Nor the warrior's gushing blood—
All should stop a while.
Death should stop.

Fazıl Hüsnü Dağlarca

To the Public Prosecutor

Prosecutor, did you ever think
What gives the hills their crowned height?
Day or night, they never hush but shout from the peak.
A jobless man from the hills stands barefoot at your door.
Even you pity his plight.

Prosecutor, did you ever think
What gives the knives their bite?
A right never claimed, bloodshed never questioned . . .
The toil and sweat of this man or that
Crowns the head and makes it bright.

Prosecutor, did you ever think
What you find in writings to indict?
Huge with mind and soul, days against the night . . .
But, down the ages, over you
What gives me all my might?

Fazıl Hüsnü Dağlarca

Quatrains

SOFT

The mouth
Of a hungry man
Makes the bread
Come alive

OF A CAT

Widows
While closing the door
Always hear
A cat going up the stairs

GOD AND I

He
Is the poet of his job
I am the God
Of mine

CATS

The widow's
Cat
Is warmer
Than the bride's cat

Fazıl Hüsnü Dağlarca

Beacon

Jutting far into the high seas, the promontory,
Cherished as the lazulite and silver night, smolders.
A terrestrial love starts in the dark
While the beacon shines
Despite destiny on the boulders.

Clouds fuse in crepuscular dimensions,
From distant harbors fogs descend,
And sadness stirs in the darkness of fate;
Blazing and blinking, the beacon inquires:
Where in life do you stand, where in love do you stand?

If the heart cringes in the starlight,
Memories might recede and recoil.
Time may tread on without the soul's cargo
As the beacon has stood for ages
With patience on this same soil.

It witnessed sea battles and ancient pirates,
Caught the wind asleep and the waves in flight,
As blue and black as a single eye,
And vacant as the vast seas;
Ill-fated fishermen struggled in its sight.

In your hair a cool air smells of salt and death,
On your face a cyclone's tastes linger.
You stand weary and forlorn,
Suddenly flickering, quivering with joy:
Something, perhaps life, is now longer.

Dolorous as the widows' indomitable desires,
Upon its prowess the gargantuan night lies.
Insane, taciturn, and awake,
It craves from disaster the charity of end-all;
It is wise.

Our drunken vessels roll and sway,
The sleep of buried hurricanes is stirred,
Rocks stretch far like pelagic graves,
From the sea to heaven
The sailor's curse is heard.

Time vanishes and life abandons time;
From the galaxies descend no bulletins.
Heavy and tired with an ill omen,
When all men are thought to have ceased,
The beacon grins.

Fazıl Hüsnü Dağlarca

Audience

I am Halim the Third, majestic and sacred,
King of Kings.
When my white hands move,
My subjects come upon their mornings.

The moments I conquer carry my lust
To unknown virgins time and again;
I discovered time in the golden pleasure
Of my enduring reign.

Along my wisdom they stretch,
All the world's dimensions;
Comfort flows from my body
Into my palaces and stately mansions.

In legion with the mighty eagles,
I set science, poetry, and victory free
So that generations to come
May rejoice on land and sea.

Dark-ridden and blue, heavens lie
At the beck and call of my head;
Poised as two infinities,
My love equals my blood.

Noble and hale, glorious and supreme,
Farther than the mind's eye can see through,
I am Halim the Third.
Mountains and rocks, who are you?

Fazıl Hüsnü Dağlarca

A Corpse Turns Cold

In the distance, the hearses came to a halt.
In a far-off temple, the candle went dead.
At midnight all the crops turned pale,
And faith left the body as in a deathbed.

Kites were soaring dawn after dawn:
The wind snatched a kite from a kid.
Climates at their loveliest, all blue:
The tallies, like a flask, were emptied.

And songs in villages, from light and toil,
Stars swimming like fish in the northern skies,
The seas whose waves give life its form
But beyond which no ocean lies.

Far away, the pounding of a brave heart,
In infidel factories, trains full of spring.
Twinkles return to the heart's remoteness
As dreams that the ultimate images bring.

Crucifixes are affirmations of eternity;
Horizons are their own lack.
It stretches into the sky as a line,
Turn the lamp off, smoke is raging black.

A mad crowd beckons and rejoices,
Thrusting in my way their hands like bony threats.
"Someone else has arrived, someone else"
O sky teeming with minarets.

Those I left behind are with me now,
The mercy, silence, and fear of hearts.
The world's wooden stairway.
In the huge barracks the guard duty starts.

Caught between the two crowds, all alone,
Homeless circles in the sky's arch.
Leaving life and death behind,
Over the fallen martyrs they march.

Memories and nights are torn asunder,
Golden streams seek to have their fate revealed.
On the children swarming like ants
Doors, huge as mountains, are sealed.

All over my face, by someone's bony fingers,
Soft soil is hurled,
Then my eyes are covered by someone else
Who is jealous of his blessed world.

Fazıl Hüsnü Dağlarca

My Translators

Night turns
Darkness into light.

    Water transforms
    The soil into green.

The hand converts
Strokes into writing.

    Science transmutes
    The sky into the earth.

The wind changes
Rocks into sculpture.

    The bird translates
    Silence into song.

Heroes transfigure
Enslavement into freedom.

Fazıl Hüsnü Dağlarca

Night of the Amnesty

Prison gates swung open with the decree of amnesty.
Out poured big noses, shaven necks, black chins,
Knees bent, shoulders deformed, backs wrenched; they rushed
Out of huge darknesses closed to time.
Huddled together they came,
Tattered, filthy, lice-covered, ugly.
The streets resounded with life, sweltering, zesty.

In amazement he ran his fingers through his hair again and again.
He had served nine years.

His mother in his arms, his child giving him hugs—
The crowd seethed in front of the prison gate.
Some had rushed all the way from mountain villages,
Some from the seas,
Their hearts clutched by a longing greater than death.
With love they looked for their very own,
Bread in their saddlebags, water in their jugs.

He couldn't believe the sight of all those streets.
He had served twenty years.

The frenzied urge that the heart exudes
Clung to the past with such ardor,
She melted away on the convict's chest.
Remorse for poplars and fields and cattle,
Remorse for ships and weddings and rivers,
Remorse from cradles and oxcarts in silence,
Not by heaven and earth but in multitudes . . .

He embraced all of us like a madman.
He had served five and a half years.

The question of those left in jail invades the blue.
From behind the iron bars,
Both happy and mourning like the wind,
A song of the native land renews the dark.
Time is not light, yet it is.
The empty wards are lying in ambush.
If you ever go back, they will torture you.

In the light his burnt-out eye grew and grew.
He had served eight years.

In bundles, the half sleep of a night or a thousand nights
Walks away from the earth when fatigue takes hold.
Out of the crowd they dispersed in ones and twos, free,
To the east and west, to the north and south, free,
An avalanche in their hearts—
Life's joys—
Life's frights.

His stricken side bobbed and throbbed.
He had served seventeen years.

Fazıl Hüsnü Dağlarca

Imperial Command

Tonight no one shall sleep in my nation:
One times one equals one thousand.
I was disturbed by the beckonings
That flared up from this calculation.

Like scientists we shall acquire the knowledge
Of the stars and darknesses by dawn.
Is it the touch of ancient sultans:
Each book has a gilded edge?

To share in the universe and its blessing
Let everyone fill his hands with rock and soil and wind
Until they all turn white
Under the sacred branches of the morning.

I know beautiful things about love and death
From the emerald ponds and marble baths.
All I know is: Soon a state shall be founded
Far greater than my country's breadth.

The imperial command that I made my town criers shout
Is all too clear on the green of the leaves;
Let him who holds his life in faith
Break the circle drawn around him by walking out.

With its huge dark letters the sky is hard to read,
I am the sultan but I am afraid just the same.
Let everyone draw his life from me tonight,
Let everyone live in my name.

Fazıl Hüsnü Dağlarca

Endless Silence

I am like a brother to you   well yes you can tell me
How you got married
How you stopped loving one night
All right you can tell me

And then in the days of that old photograph
Your mother had not gone mad yet
Your hair was golden as it caressed your white shoulders
All right you can tell me

You used to laugh a lot
At trees
You were a sylph   the forest kept you awake when it sprouted
All right you can tell me

Then you ran away from home
To thoughts solitude sleep death
Stark-naked among the ruins of a fire
All right you can tell me

A girl a boy   stone shadows on the walls   a girl a boy
Three hundred youths you had slept in a mountain shelter
Outside the snow was cold as wolves   in your heart you froze like the Stone Age
All right you can tell me

Look tomorrow I am leaving for another darkness
Like cemeteries I am silent mournful deaf
Yes you no longer have faith in love   yes you will love no one ever again
All right you can tell me

Fazıl Hüsnü Dağlarca

Return

Soldiers are returning, aged soldiers
From the blue hills of peace.
How intimate within our hearts
What their steps would not release . . .

Songs are returning, songs of light
Sung on bulky oxcarts.
Are the gardens across a mirror
Some new destiny that starts?

Birds are returning, loyal birds,
For our eaves, not for the sake of spring.
We come alive in the whirling distance
And the beauty that the seasons bring.

Ships are returning, strange and opulent,
Sailing the strange and endless seas.
In the depths, like beams of light,
The cargo of the ships tarries.

Unlike any of these, my night,
You, you are returning into my hands.
I am returning to love and life
From all the dead of all the lands.

Fazıl Hüsnü Dağlarca

I Am Listening to Istanbul

I am listening to Istanbul, intent, my eyes closed:
At first there is a gentle breeze
And the leaves on the trees
Softly sway;
Out there, far away,
The bells of water-carriers unceasingly ring;
I am listening to Istanbul, intent, my eyes closed.

I am listening to Istanbul, intent, my eyes closed;
Then suddenly birds fly by,
Flocks of birds, high up, with a hue and cry,
While the nets are drawn in the fishing grounds
And a woman's feet begin to dabble in the water.
I am listening to Istanbul, intent, my eyes closed.

I am listening to Istanbul, intent, my eyes closed.
The Grand Bazaar's serene and cool,
An uproar at the hub of the Market,
Mosque yards are full of pigeons.
While hammers bang and clang at the docks
Spring winds bear the smell of sweat;
I am listening to Istanbul, intent, my eyes closed.

I am listening to Istanbul, intent, my eyes closed;
Still giddy from the revelries of the past,
A seaside mansion with dingy boathouses is fast asleep.
Amid the din and drone of southern winds, reposed,
I am listening to Istanbul, intent, my eyes closed.

I am listening to Istanbul, intent, my eyes closed.
A pretty girl walks by on the sidewalk:
Four-letter words, whistles and songs, rude remarks;
Something falls out of her hand—
It's a rose, I guess.
I am listening to Istanbul, intent, my eyes closed.

I am listening to Istanbul, intent, my eyes closed.
A bird flutters round your skirt;
On your brow, is there sweat? Or not? I know.
Are your lips wet? Or not? I know.
A silver moon rises beyond the pine trees:
I can sense it all in your heart's throbbing.
I am listening to Istanbul, intent, my eyes closed.

Orhan Veli Kanık

For You

For you, my fellow humans,
Everything is for you,
Nights are for you, days are for you;
Daylight is for you, moonlight is for you;
Leaves in the moonlight,
Wonder and wisdom in the leaves,
Myriad greens in daylight,
Yellow is for you, and pink.
The feel of the skin on the palm,
Its warmth,
Its softness,
The comfort of lying down;
For you are all the greetings
And the masts swaying in the harbor;
Names of the days,
Names of the months,
Fresh paint on rowboats is for you,
Mailmen's feet,
Potters' hands,
Sweat on foreheads,
Bullets fired on battlefronts;
Graves are for you and tombstones,
Jails and handcuffs and death sentences
Are for you.
Everything is for you.

Orhan Veli Kanık

This World

This world drives you out of your mind,
This night, these stars, this fragrance,
This tree bursting with flowers from tip to toe.

Orhan Veli Kanık

Living

I

I know living isn't an easy thing to do
Or falling in love and singing of your girl
Taking a stroll under the stars at night
Warming up in the sunshine by day
Sneaking out for half a day to take it easy
On top of Istanbul's loveliest hill
—Countless shades of blue flow in the Bosphorus—
And to forget all in the legions of blue.

II

I know living isn't an easy thing to do
But look
The bed of a dead man is still warm,
A dead man's wristwatch is ticking.
Brother, living is no easy affair,
But dying isn't easy, either.

Leaving the world isn't easy at all.

Orhan Veli Kanık

Exodus

I

From his window overlooking the roofs
The harbor was in sight
Church bells
Tolled all day long.
From his bed the trains could be heard
From time to time
And at night.
He loved a girl
Who lived in the house across the street.
Be that as it may,
He left this town
And moved to another.

II

Now the poplars are in view
Out of his window
Along the canal.
Daytime it keeps raining
And the moon is up at night.
There's a market in the square nearby.
As for him, all the time,
Whatever it is—a trip or money or a letter,
He keeps thinking of something.

Orhan Veli Kanık

For Our Homeland

All the things we did for this land of ours!
Some of us died;
Some of us gave speeches.

Orhan Veli Kanık

Just for the Hell of It

All the pretty women thought
The poems I wrote on love
Were meant for them.
And I always felt badly
About having written them
Just for the hell of it.

Orhan Veli Kanık

The Flute

When he likened the cemetery to a herd of sheep
Or the day he felt like it, he wrote on a piece of paper:
"Death is to join the herd." And yet there was
Neither cemetery nor flute nor shepherd in this assertion.
The sound of the flute came from afar, light and playful.
The whistle had plunged into silence when it returned
To the grave saying, "Here are the shepherds!" Sheep stirred.
All this, he never wrote down, but buried—better that way—
In a single line: "Death is to join the herd."
Now the flute played for him alone, but it can suddenly stop.

Oktay Rifat

A Formidable Gypsy

Peeling a willow branch, a formidable gypsy
Made a whistle in a two-horse buggy.
We swooped down on the tents in the meadow
Stealthily, with zinc and daisies;
A sunny wind blew, the air was warm.

Along roads that slope down in view of the sea,
Flanked by mallow and patience dock,
Recline on the wet grass if you like or walk around.
A sheep dog trailed us step by step,
Then stopped, peed, sniffed the roots of the shrubs.

With the softest breeze, my tree stirs,
The crow lets itself go down to the ground
Like lightning from atop a pine tree, my heart throbs.
The sky, just a few clouds, evening sadness—
What else is there left to us in this false world?

Oktay Rifat

On the Nomad Sea

I

You and I, and our flowerpot on the balcony:
Busybee Elizabeth. The building's first triangle.

Neither old nor new. As if the most lucid
Moment of our destiny is trembling

On the nomad sea. We're not aware of it.
The sound of the rock resembles the human voice.

At a glimpse you find out: The flowerpot
On the balcony has replaced the cloud. The clouds

Turn themselves into horses in all that foam.
You and I keep running, ahead of us

A red bird shakes the ancient elder tree
A blind child was looking at a moment ago.

Then the cloud turns into the flowerpot again,
Horses begin to heave, we rest, in our ears

A murmur lingers like indecipherable words
Spoken by the walls. Out of this day, this morning.

II

Not to remember, not to forget. Where the ends meet,
Along the crimson smells of the shores,

Growing like the trills of a crippled nightingale,
In the heavy and slow symbols of our gaze.

And I emigrate to you moment by moment
I return, in an exodus, like a vibration,

Seeking the rocks of your lips,
Seeking your name which I wrote in rain.

Now you vanish in the crevices of your own valley,
Now you gush out

All over your vanished valley.
Time and again I am lost to myself.

This is all there is to it. Neither old nor new
Like the most lucid moment of our destiny.

Countless blue transforming into a thought
Unused as those words which cannot exist alone,

Which emerge out of nowhere;
The soul is a coal crystal, rises out of darkness

Like a scarlet moon, and watches over the night.
And pioneering the numerical shapes,

It closes in on all things that scatter
And come together, like a carnivorous plant.

Scattering is none other than coming together.
The sexual fluid that breaks out of its shell,

The sun's taut, then loosened, bow, first images
Of the starry oysters twinkling.

The sky's wing turning red and growing pale;
All sorts of fruit on branches, feet sealed,

Sprouting frantically to a new infinity, then falling;
The soil whose panting like a sea lion

Moves us deep down, full of bleached bones.
Neither old nor new. That's all there is to it.

That is all. You and I and our flowerpot on the balcony.
Alone in the fluttering of heavy symbols.

III

There. I sprinkle all the words by the handfuls
To the birds, to the roots of roses,

To the lip of the sun, to the skirt
Of the prancing morning, to the red velvet of rocks,

To the moon's horns, and to the honeysuckle
Hanging out of the railing of your hair . . .

All by myself I cast my image over all shapes
And over the cross-eyed bottoms of the seas.

IV

Henry Moore is busy picking up pebbles on the beach,
Little fertile, some with holes in the middle,

Just like the women's teats, like figs,
Dreams on their shoulders.

The heart is meant for the wisdom that no form
Is doomed to suffering.

Rocks that ennoble the world, with lodes, slab by slab,
Wave like flags that have wiped

The bloodstains of being alive.
Bones, all those human bones and animal bones,

The daintiest and the mightiest wreaths
Of the passage from one shape to another.

And the seashells, grooved inside out,
Smell of shadows like the forehead of a billy goat.

Delight was meant to cross
Animals and grass.

All those trunks of trees covered
With graffiti like the walls of the mad . . .

The locked gem of the birds
Transforming the dead into the stars.

Man craved more, so much more.
All the more. Neither old nor new.

Perhaps it is a giant that dies and is resurrected
Time and again or a goddess frightened to death

These mute monuments which bloom like flowers
With their helter-skelter lines to the eye.

The eye is the god of its own harmony,
Segment by segment, against and opposite the whole.

Shape turning into shape, the resounding water
Of the present, life's alarm clock;

The enigmatic masts of change, the shriek,
The diamond of action, woman, noun, and verb.

Like a bull that dashes through a village
I shooed away whatever you had in you.

Now I know how hard it is to divest oneself
Of a two-dimensional raid and to live in a blue moment.

If the eye that sees is the eye that is seen
Then I am someone else.

This framework belongs neither to yesterday nor to tomorrow.
Tomorrow is an image, so is yesterday.

The sea, the bird, the wind, the rain
Belong to this day, this morning.

V

Freud is seated in the subconscious of a tree,
He keeps poking the dreams of the earth.

There are poppies that brighten these dreams.
Sea, bird, wind, rain.

The dream, a star distilled late
From action's bed of milky figs,

Late or early, the fish that leaps suddenly
Out of yesterday's waters;

A scarlet turmoil that has turned daylight inside out,
The face of a cramped well asleep and awake.

Epochs seem hidden in seeds,
Swings creaking in the soil.

Sea, bird, rain, wind.
And I found myself crucified

Between the past and the future, like a dream.
Neither old nor new. As if the most lucid

Moment of our destiny is trembling
In the waters of the sea laid waste.

Melih Cevdet Anday

Startling Encounter

"I had lived this moment a long time ago,"
You say in amazement.
A house you entered for the first time, the stairs,
The window that suddenly gets the sun,

And the train whistle right on time . . .
That is the way these colors and sounds
Came together some day just before noon
When you were not in the world yet.

Or, is living remembering?
I don't think so, maybe we too were just a sound
For some people on that bygone
Startling encounter.

Melih Cevdet Anday

The Flower of Darkness

I set foot on the soil of this world
as if I was making love to a sleeping woman
The hot bees of my eyes kept landing
on the bushes of silence and flying off again
All for nothing their feet were covered with flowerdust

I am unrelenting pain the trees are deaf
Dawn's distilled steel is no comfort for me
All for nothing day arrives its lances
cannot hoodwink me I have read
the fable of land and sea
the simple tale of birth and death

I found the Flower of Darkness in the forest
like the blindman's armband with three dots
The sea's desolate banner is all for nothing
The bird that carries the vision to its nest
The moon's padlock over the sky all for nothing

Melih Cevdet Anday

Are We Going To Live Without Aging?

At dawn, a throng came out
Of the skies: Convex shields, glittering
Tattoos, a rose, a daggered
Heart, bows of wheat,
Aquariums emptying out, a king,
A turkey's crest, a fresh corpse,
Brass-footed horses, and wine in a glazed jug
Waiting to be poured into the sea.
A tumult arose from the roots of the trees,
Eyeless monsters emerged from the sea.
What's that? Should we believe in rapacious beaks?
Or in thin axes, in grass burned at night
Or in tree-shaped wings?
I pay no heed to clouds, I don't care
If they go south along the river
Or to the slow lakes set afire by towers.
Let them go . . . Are we going to live without aging?
Come, let's go and see the dawn's spider.

Melih Cevdet Anday

Vertigo

From a sea in bloom everything will burst
One day and be a forest.
From now on what you'll see is the soft hour
Of birds on the branches where they rest.
Wait for the god who waits around:
On blood-red pines, the sun
Will claw till the great night comes on.

One day, all will be sound, such sound
As travels from star to cloud and to star from earthly things,
So its ellipse will spread with resounding chimes.
While you eye these rings,
Wait for the voice among voices to rebound.
Passing through organ music, the hair-winged moon
Will come out quite soon.

I have lived in the wind.
Vertigo turned into lonely day. Alone,
My prophets were far-off rocks.
Neither forest nor sound, all by myself, windblown
Rain comforts the soul.
If not, godlike we must wait around
To hear a voice or any sound.

Melih Cevdet Anday

Copper Age

A raven crowed without knowing why.
Faster. On a pine tree which must wait.
Our familiar summer arrived on one wing,
Not even weary, inept and lonesome.
Let's make believe we see for the first time,
Not to upset the rule. Faster.

Thinking is half of speed.
Faster. Summer should come sooner,
Winter sooner, mid-month and the child.
Concerts and ulcers, love and government
And balding, the clock should run faster
So must death . . . Faster.

Death is nature's being one-eyed.
Graves should be dug round. Faster.
Dead men were rotund in the Copper Age.
We must call loneliness nature's timidity
And death the effort to affirm the self, oh
The fear of being forgotten. Faster.

Speed is half of nature, the other half
Is death. Which means faster.
Like summer it comes without knowing why.
We must die as if it's the first time,
Not to upset the rule. Faster.
We must stall.

Nature is half of man.
Death is all of speed.
—Today or tomorrow.
One might just as soon die today. Faster,
Better too.
You might have died yesterday.

—Yesterday a hot wind blew,
Remember, the kids went to the movies,
My morning tea toppled on the tablecloth.

—Today and tomorrow are the same,
Either a hot wind blows or the tea topples.
Why are you looking at the kids, they might all die.
Peace and war are one.
Nature and man are the same.
Speed and death are one.

A raven crowed without knowing why
On top of a pine tree which must wait.
Nothing matters except the laws, said somebody,
Man does not concern me, never magnify death.

Someone bewildered about summer's arrival
Asked himself if life is guilt.

Melih Cevdet Anday

The Battle of Kadesh[1]

On one of the banks of the River Orontes
Mutawallis stood among his soldiers
And stared without stirring.
On the opposite bank, the Pharaoh
Ramses had mounted his chariot:
He stared straight ahead.
This is all we know about it.
Even though history tells it at length
This look is all that remains or can remain.

Melih Cevdet Anday

1. Kadesh is the ancient city (in present-day Syria) that was the site of the famous Battle of Kadesh (1274 B.C.) in which the powerful Egyptian Pharaoh Ramses II was defeated by the troops of King Mutawallis of the Hittite Empire with its capital at Boğazköy (in eastern Turkey).

From: Odysseus Bound

PART II, SECTION 5

It is neither cloud nor leaf that goes
For a color grows big like a thought.
My hand is there so I can't hold the bough.
After gazing I forgot my eyes in the sea,
For the sky slowly turns into my memory,
No sense nor sight only the stars now.
Am I whole or a fragment, who knows?
Loaded with suns I am lost and gone;
Neither the earth is lost nor the sun.

PART II, SECTION 6

I scampered in an array out of kilter:
As I ran my loneliness was on the rise,
I stared out of a dinotherium's eyes
At myself—what folly!—alien in space.
A seagull that had rooted out the sea
Now kept swinging it on its beak;
Latched on to a bird the wind got feathery,
Growing denser at a slow pace
The thunder shortly became the tree.

PART III, SECTION 3

I had never seen these hands of mine
For they used to be my trees
Should I turn off the light now and
Get up to grab hold of my trees
Are they my hands or the names
Of my hands? Right now I am also
An achromatic color, a declaration;
What is early summer but the fact

Of early summer? The extraordinary
Quaintness of ordinary shapes
Is due to their revival like the soil.

PART III, SECTION 7

If words are motionless in the middle of the orbit
What after all is growth without movement
"This is the mythology of modern death"[1]
Order apart from form, shape apart from mold
Consonance on the one hand, congruence on the other
It is not existence nor death, but the other one.
The voice between sound and quiet
Conviction without knowledge, science without faith
Substance somewhere and essence somewhere else
Feeling without sensation, sentiment without sense
Poised between the real and the ideal.

Melih Cevdet Anday

1. Line by Wallace Stevens.

Time of Death

Who says death—and though the fingers point out
Death goes away empty-handed.

One better be rich if he is to stay long.
For as we shrink we must diminish,
And then during clean and brief illnesses . . .

In the old days one could stay a little longer
In the attic without being noticed;
Nowadays if fidgety people are waiting in line
You must vacate the mattresses as soon as you can.

For it is terrible if it goes on.

Behçet Necatigil

Limit

Often it was out of boredom that we fell
Into friendship and love and the streets
Where a road roller would crush us flat
At the end perhaps . . .

Hair and mirrors, and everything else
Receded and vanished. Our fall,
With the bow pulled and released,
Was surefire after all.

Hoops turn loose and muscles melt away;
Life's only meaning is paradox.
On pensive papers we search
What used to be there some day.

What is it we hide from
When they ring our doorbell?
But they get zero times loneliness
If they add up all of us.

Behçet Necatigil

Dark Dominion

Stabbed by the most malicious of men,
Bleeding, the world fell into the darkest abyss;
Smothering the days of frenzy
Along endless distances,
Night broke loose in an avalanche
Off the mighty mountain.

All voices deserted the street
All houses fell asleep
An infant wept sucking his mother's white breasts
Full of fate's black milk;
The eyes of the corpses
Stared petrified and sad.

Behçet Necatigil

A Story of the Sea

We shall always swim together in these blue waters
In this vervain sea that resembles your face.
Beating together, both my pulse and yours
Will strike at death and denounce darkness.

All the fish will chase us from the depths,
Saying Külebi is here now with his loved one.
Like a gull swooping from the vast horizon
The wind will drop shafts of light like pearls.

And the pearls will glitter around your neck,
On your chest and arms, like the words of my verses,
Sea anemone on your hair, your most secret parts,
Like rain, the stars will glide in your eyes.

Our love shall make these blue flames sacred.

Cahit Külebi

Dead

I

ON THE FRONTIERS OF PAIN

The dead write their names in caps
On the walls of a room riddled with holes.

Casting my shadow very long
In two letters.

Heart and soul, ears are listening to water
Because it's fresh blood
And it will leave its place
To the shore of a revolt.

II

DEATH

Has death changed its character or what?
It scratches itself out

In a denial of its self.
Its blood.

Its blood trickling with greater speed
And gathering.

Fire is now rising to its feet
Because death has been arrested.

III

ON THE WAY OUT

The dead:
"Who darkened the sky like this?"
Saying: "Put this question
To the poet."

On the shore of pain
On the way out.

This is one of the questions to be asked.

IV

Death was watched.

İlhan Berk

For Homer

I

Homer led a tranquil life. Like mountain roads.
Quietly he prepared himself—the way
water is ready to flow
for the principles of poetry.

Like all the great poets of the world
he studied bird and beast, the raging sea
and the first flames and flashes of the day.

That is why Homer resembles Homer alone.

II

We know Homer as the master of long poems
And long suffering.
Thus on this globe
His long robe and high stature went and came back.

İlhan Berk

The Critics

They know their English:
The Victorian Age,
Eliot schmeliot
Are complete on their shelves.

They know their French:
From its origins to the present
The grasshopper and the ant
From La Fontaine to our day.

I am not even mentioning
Those who know Italian and German
The erudite scholars
Those who do it the American way.

Bookworms!
When I open the windows,
In the bazaar, at the café, in the sun's garden
Turkish is a lively rose.

They smell poetry as fruit vendors
Smell the rear end of melons
To find out
If they are ripe or not.

They forbid you
The heart's most natural right
Which is to sing sincere songs
In the mother tongue.

They set strict rules and laws
The bugs of taste in chests
Eating away at life's fabric,
Worms nibbling away at the core of poetry.

They are the bigwigs,
Like cabinet members
Or congressmen who live it up
And dupe poetry at every election.

Ceyhun Atuf Kansu

The Daily Rose

Unless they carry the news of spring days
All the newspapers had better be closed
And unless the type metal smells of rose
All the pages ought to come out blank.

He who knows not the rose should not govern;
No one should talk of social order and what not
If the people forsake the time of the rose
And abandon the sagging acacia to rot.

They are the only true friends of the seasons:
From heavenly gardens a grade-school girl descends
Holding the loveliest of orders in her hands
A red rose and a white rose.

Living is the oldest of all constitutions:
Blood is a rose, joy is a rose, love is a rose,
And bread is a rose awakened at daybreak;
So the headlines of daily papers should read:
Beam like a rose, laugh like a rose, be a rose.

Ceyhun Atuf Kansu

Geography Lesson

The subject of today's lesson is geography
Don't be wary at all to go near the guys
There Bolu[1] forests are straight ahead
Take a love stroll early in the morning
Don't be bashful our subject is geography

Look this is the place they call Asia
Here's Beyoğlu Avenue this is in Hong Kong
Watch your step don't crush the Chinese
Stuff the yellowest of them into your bag
Don't forget our subject is geography

I could tell this was going to happen
See you smashed the Calcutta elephants
Hold it now climb the Himalayas at least
Take off your clothes on the Tibet plateau
Don't be shy our subject is geography

Miss you aren't listening to our lecture
Look these are the sultans of Africa
Who tirelessly eat pineapple four seasons
Well love your Ethiopian lads if you like
Don't be ashamed our subject is geography

And these here are the Alps
Don't say you can't see for all those men
Going down you have the Venetian counts
Go to sleep in the streets of Rome at noon
Don't forget our subject is geography

1. Bolu: A mountainous province in western Turkey.

Now look this is the sea of Paris
Held in the hands of Queen Brigitte Bardot
And higher up you have the Bank of England
High time you made off with the sterling
Don't be scared our subject is geography

That's all for today some other time
We'll see the United States with Texas Rangers
But go ahead hug your husbands right away
I guess your husbands won't mind it either
Don't forget our subject is geography

Salâh Birsel

Old Night

Our sadness
Is a half-open door
Standing there a pitcher and a cat.

The mountain isn't there
But its shadow
Is still on the wall.

Our lamp is covered with soot
We turn it down gently
And leave it in a corner of the balcony.

Sabahattin Kudret Aksal

Mozart's Birds

The clock strikes nine
He will spend the morning at the piano
As sparrows cheerfully chirp outside
Skipping from this branch to that
With his eyes on the light-filled window
When his fingers coddle the keys
A little sonata by Mozart begins
Sparrows break into silence
The light glittering on the walls
Are all Mozart's now
And the birds that chirp in the glare
Are Mozart's birds

For two years each morning this little sonata
Each morning with a new meaning
Like life itself ceaselessly glowing and gleaning
A life better and nicer and more real
Casts aside our obscure abstruse speech
And we listen to ourselves like water and leaves

Weary of obsession and worry
To believe and to hope anew
Not free of the heart's swift disillusion
In the night's silence
Or in distant meadows in the morning
To find and to lose Mozart

Necati Cumalı

Aphorisms

POINT

I'd have taken it if she told me lies.
Instead she told me a lie.

BOUND

Make me believe in such a lie
That its truth may last all my life.

THE HITCH

Some day,
If they say everyone into his own garden,
Will you be ready?

JURY

All colors gathered dirt at the same speed:
They gave the first prize to white.

Özdemir Asaf

Ancient Sea Folk

Fifteen men on a dead man's chest
Yo-ho-ho and a bottle of rum!
Drink and the devil had done for the rest
Yo-ho-ho and a bottle of rum! [1]

pebbles chant an odd song there and the sea shepherds
drive their herds into the high seas
while on the mussels' iris harlot blues crouch
in the boundless western time's green galleons
unforgettable and emerald and sighted
blood-drenched slab by slab
you hear the ancient sea folk in harbor taverns
those kinky sea people if you listen
spanish songs and italian wine
and godlike you create curses
from fifteen meridian to twenty you create universal curses
atop the mainmast
you god of blasphemy and tumult and of my enigma
you god of lost treasures
you shall not look behind nor spit at the wind
unless black flags are hoisted on the admiral's mast
no honest breeze shall spark your corsair's eyes
unless you chew on the rain or on tobacco

I never forgot the mediterranean
I plunged into flames and wept voraciously
the joy of creating
and being created flared tremulously in the sky
and prayers burst open like titanic sails
then lo and behold three crescents arose at once

1. From Robert Lewis Stevenson, *Treasure Island.*

barbarossa[2] songs released like hawks from their arms
cyclone-sized barefoot mariners of the algerian skipper
who arrested the caravans of ships
and held the straits of messina and septe and all others
there is no god but God
arrested and set all the vessels on fire
fire's joyous and memorable dominion
stirs in constellations and beacons isthmus by isthmus
then bound for rome in legion with hannibal
the phoenicians carried the alphabet and glass long ago
dragons breathed fire and the avatars of the sea monsters
and the ghost of a genoese galley slave haunted a rhodes castle
his feet shackled
a dagger stuck in his back
while latin songs poured forth
from the vessels of antonius

you unexpected unforgettable unbearable and deep
and magnified
as roguish as a cabin boy or a sailor's mustache
the wind uncontained in its rose and in its own dimensions
the centuries-old buccaneer fate of yours
tattooed on your arms and infinitely on your chest
green and speckled
angel-faced mermaids and unctuous dolphins
you sense from the world what the children sense
while time keeps aging you remain a child
you are the ancient sea cemetery of pirates and sailors
the graveyard of barbarossa songs
with your mighty waves you are the ocean
the starry multitudes of the plankton and the skate
you are god and bear gods in your kingdom

2. "Barbarossa" Hayreddin Pasha: Admiral of the Ottoman fleet in the reign of Sultan Süleyman the Magnificent (sixteenth century).

the master skippers who tyrannize the currents and eddies
cruise north-northeast and some cruise westward
there once was captain joy whom we buried in the iceberg sea
an andersen and a kidd
a salih a burak and a memi[3]
together exploding our laughter as cannons in salvo
at a giants' carnival
swayed and scattered we had died
then the fish garths near the shores and archipelagos
being so ancient and stately as to defy memory
forsaking all the stars to recognize the north star at one glance
italian fishermen with beards dripping with salt
then as in purgatory raveled and fibrous
to disembark sahara-parched at a port where foxes spit copper
and to come aboard truculent in a deluge of wine
blessed be thy name
whenever we cruise toward the south pole
from tierra del fuego
from the flameland

Attilâ İlhan

3. Salih, Burak, Memi: Ottoman naval heroes.

The Dead Have Grown Old

the downpour of stars is no less than a servile salute
lilies are white and whites are no less than lilies
over the marshes mosquitoes multiply by the million
bugs and insects are linked forever in hug and embrace
the downpour of stars is no less than a servile salute

all the old equestrians spur the wayworn up the hill
sweltering in galaxies horses will burst inside out
on hoary battlefields lie the wounded and the martyred
pines and willows are linked forever in hug and embrace
should a girl come alive or a mortal die or a star fall
all the old equestrians spur the wayworn up the hill

hyenas refuse to recall the saturnalia and all
life's flight from the body and man's from humanity
a hundred killed a hundred orphaned a hundred lost
mothers raise their sons for combat overseas
hyenas refuse to recall the saturnalia and all
should a girl come alive or a mortal die or a star fall
whoever is dead is dead and the dead have grown old

Attilâ İlhan

Captain

I never knew you had violet eyes

I am weary of living the midnight

you forgot your hands in the palm of the chilly air
and failed to recognize me though I walked by you
it's true I've changed a lot I have a beard and all
my poems flutter about like ashen pigeons
and I lost patience with those copper skies
Paris skies just drive me insane
reminding me of you and the Poitiers girl before you

you forgot your hands in the palm of the chilly air

beyond darkness spark-eyed whores linger
leaning on their shadows they wait like saints

you shall stop when the red light goes on

it's true I've changed a lot I have a beard and all
your chilly eyes gathered mist you couldn't have known me
even Ricardo exiled stateless Ricardo
passed by right under my nose without recognizing me
and yet we had been together day and night at *au vieux châtelet*
the three of us used to drink Viennese coffee and hot rum
he adored *Krapfen* which is supposed to be nice
I never could figure out why he liked it anyway

now I want to be alone redeemed from loneliness itself

I lost sight of you near the Montmartre metro station
I paid no attention whether that black man was behind you
or not with a squalid whistle on his lips like a cigarette

chewing and spitting jazz tunes by Sidney Bechet
no matter how he tries to hide it I know he's in love with you
the color of his face is the avatar of all his sorrows

I picked up a newspaper but I'll read it when I get home

I wish I could go into a café and order a grog
and devise a plot to murder you
silence frosty and frozen white on my mustache
I shall remain tight-lipped like a proud totem
I wish my song will be lost the fretful song of silence
and I will be lost and all my poems
those I wrote for you and for everyone else
should be forsaken like bygone sultans
I would forget you never remember you never
I wish I'll never recall your betrayal and your lust
my hands should forget you irretrievably once and for all
a black man stares milk-white through midnight
at rue lafayette I pass from yesterday into today

I forgot your violet eyes in a glass of grog

Attilâ İlhan

Another Man

They'd better leave her alone
unmolested
that blind Alsatian woman
who plays polkas by heart on her harmonica
the girl in whom the songs start and end
had better go along the Boulevard Raspail each night
just leave her alone
that woman who plays the harmonica
when the lights vanish some night
don't drag me behind the walls
don't drag her away

the drugged clouds of the Zuider Zee
haunt his memory
while a Dutch painter
paints nothing but turquoise skies
from dawn to dusk
on the quay of Orfèvre
kids drift along the shore of a song
their hands cleansed pure in the rain
barefoot and dreamy-eyed
their laughter endless their tears unwept

I saw the stars scuttling along the seashore
their irises were ridged deep
with flaming lines
while the south wind blew
and the north wind gushed
I shivered

beyond all enormity
as the beacons stared into darkness like orphans
on the coast of Palermo and Calabria
sailors stood on decks vagrant and sad

with melancholy eyes
unknown
unseen
unfelt
on the coast of Palermo and Calabria
the beacons stared
into darkness like orphans
and I the poet of the anvil and the wrench
poured forth righteous poems
humane poems
line by line
as one would cast lead
all the way from Istanbul to Marseilles

wind in the boulevards
wind in the Luxembourg gardens
kids toss the last leaves in the air
and down below
like the pulse-beat of another world
miners' hammers clang and subways scurry like baby moles
and the harmonica sounds timid
and distant

on the pavements the sights of Paris linger
and in the sky now swift
now open
a fast blue
fast clouds
red birds are embroidered on your mittens
and sky and the pavements you and Paris
you and Paris my love
and each singing a different tune
those trips and farewells

in Ubangi-Shari
under virgin stars

in pure and honest eyes
within four walls cityless and unradioed
and our fire's five-headed flames
amid an unsurpassed adulation
fiercely and savagely
the wildest ivies burn

then a man
shoulders
the susurrant forest
the arrogant howls of jackals
and the jackals themselves
a greasy jet-black man
with a greasy pitch-black kinky beard

I am a man
another man
a vagabond
who dumped his youth headlong into the streets
and tossed away his hopes like pigeons
lost them time and time again
lost them in the graveyard of ships
in his cruel poems and songs
found them time and time again
then he dragged the dawn's shrieks by the hair
there goes the sea and there goes he
there goes the cloud and there goes he
a man
a different man
a vagabond

Attilâ İlhan

History Lesson at the Flea Market

If you recline on this brocaded couch
And if I go sit on that shelf of turbans,
Do you think we might upset the venerable dust?
If we take a pinch out of this snuffbox,
Which probably belonged to some Grand Mufti,
Do you think we might sneeze,
With the parable of the snuff long since gone?

Is this the end of the auction or just about?
After all, no more bids are to be heard.
Before the gavel sounded to announce Mr. N.
The owner of a full-length gold-leaf mirror
And before he could even say, "It's all done,"
Before his new piece jibed with the new features,
Mr. N., his mirror, his comb, and his auburn locks
All turned to dust and were scattered to the wind.
Is this the end of the auction or just about?

Were you ever, while sitting at a train window,
By the drifting trees and the earth and the rocks,
Deep in thought, watching the images of your face
With the twitches on your mouth and whatnot,
Jabbed and jostled by the rude elbow
Of some guy breezing through the corridor?

Did you then wish you were the only passenger?
Dismissing all that you wistfully watched—
The trees, the earth, the rocks, and yourself
Out of the window of the speeding train,
Did you wish you were left behind there
Where you had seen your image reflected?

Surely you have wished for that, haven't we all?

How about me buying you a mirror,
A full-length mirror with a gold-leaf frame
With the inscription on top "Here lies the deceased"?
And then we'll have your body washed clean
And in your memory we'll send out trays of fritters.

Surely you have wished for that, haven't we all?

Mr. N. had the urge to get off before the train stopped.
Yet these are venerable secondhand mirrors
And venerable mirrors fall into disuse,
With dust upon dust, and dust inside dust,
Venerable mirrors have fallen into disuse.

No one may get off while the train is moving;
If you do, they won't wash you the right way,
But they'll bury you at the flea market before you rot.

Surely you have wished for that, haven't we all?

Whatever remains after you are gone
Or whatever has remained after Mr. N. was gone
In a handful of dust,
Was it the unlived portion of his life?
Or whatever has remained after Mr. N. was gone
In a handful of dust,
Was it his death in defiance of dying?

They won't let you get off while the train is moving;
If you do, they won't wash you the right way,
They'll bury you at the flea market before you rot.

They won't allow you to mellow like wine
Or become an old man in the shade of a plane tree;
You shall remain idle in the midst of the mirrors
With dust upon dust, a passenger on the train,

Neither within the entrance nor without,
A flea market shopper with flea market items for sale.
If you live, you shall live with the dead at best,
Neither within the entrance nor without,
If you die, you shall die with death itself.

If you recline on this brocaded couch
And if I go sit on that shelf of turbans,
Do you think we might upset the venerable dust?
If we take a pinch out of this snuffbox,
Which probably belonged to some Grand Mufti,
Do you think we might sneeze,
With the parable of the snuff long since gone?

Can Yücel

The Left Ear of the Grand Vizier

It itches: the left ear of His Lordship the Grand Vizier
Like nobody's business itches that ear
The Grand Vizier is a most eminent peer
He thinks about the nation sitting here

Now itching is a function of the ear
And thinking behooves the Grand Vizier
Yet it so happens that in our land
What itches is the Grand Vizier
And who thinks is the left ear

Ümit Yaşar Oğuzcan

The Big Tale

Two Sultans—Murad I and II—
Fell at Kosovo and, as martyrs, became glorified.
Carbuncles shoved Selim the Grim to the other side.
It was a blood clot that finished Süleyman the Magnificent off.
As for Bayezid the Thunderbolt and Sultan Aziz, suicide.

From afflictions like cirrhosis and TB
Selim the Sallow, Murad IV, and Mahmud II died.
Mehmed the Conqueror, Young Osman, and Selim the Poet
Were victims of regicide.

Ahmed III, Mehmed III, and Osman III,
Mustafa II, Mahmud I, and Abdülhamid I
Suffered apoplexy, that's how they went by the wayside.
As for Abdülhamid II and Sultan Reşad,
Each had a weak heart.

And so on with all those majestic rulers—
The glorious Ottoman Empire,
On whose realm the sun never set for 624 years,
Kept the whole world petrified:

It was a legend, it died.

Nüzhet Erman

And Came the Tailors

And came the tailors. With nooks and crannies that resembled big
broken things
on darker colors over wider links
With nooks and crannies that frighten a city and put it to shame.
Fabrics were provided and the sleeping cats were patted. Then
the endless music of joylessness.
In late afternoon some went out for tea and some to the parks
Conformity shortened their days with a grief which neither grew nor
diminished.
Tired and pale, they found the fabrics and filled the city
Carrying here the ten-thousand-year-old wreath
Having buried their dead ones, they came in a crowd without brushing
off their dust
All the avenues were suddenly vacated, everybody made way,

> "Devout women and republicans
> sweepstakes sellers and flower buyers
> fishermen gathered their nets and seines and hooks and
> hoods and bags and scoops.
> Smokers threw their cigarettes on the ground and put them out."

Under thick fabrics that never warmed up, there was something they cut
and measured
Making out patterns and matching them
They cut out the end of an unbearable sleep
And broke into a requiem for a horse now dead
They did not put down their scissors
They had been expected.

> "The horse now dead—they said—
> How lovely was your folly within reach!
> You opened up
> The solitary source of thirty-three thousand breeds.

Dark sparkling mane. Your harness
—rubbed and shined with aromatic oils—
went so well with your rump and the sky.

Your endless shape gave the sky a new grandeur.
We rubbed your hoofs with filaments
And your gallop, painted black,
Awakened all the lands and all the seas.
Next to infinity we heard your frenzied neigh
Black horse, you had such lovely eyes.
Thousands of people
—children, men, women, everyone—
in splendid or slovenly clothes
blind men and lepers
and the whole crowd of the holy books
the seer and the accursed and the sinner
pregnant women and preachers
ice-cream vendors and acrobats on horseback
traders and royalists and seamen
atheists and pawnbrokers
and apostles . . .
hailing from forests and seashores and barren places
they filled your merry meadows
and shouted
Amid colossal sounds you galloped by . . ."

And came the tailors. The suns went out of the rooms now.
In the houses everyone was trembling and fidgety, trembling and fidgety
No dailies carried the news. We had embarked on an age of shops
Hundreds of tailors shut their windows in hundreds of rooms
Their fingers, slender, withered, their faces pale and old from their
standing still
Lost watch chains, trembling and fidgety, their legs tired
They acquiesced with standing still that directed all they had
they felt pleased and smiled.

"The horse now dead—they said—
Your saddle was so pretty.
Made out of a she-goat's skin, adorned with the gold of Ophir
It went so well with the noble curves of your torso
With you reflected beyond.
Beyond the sensitivity of fava beans and beets
The unattainable personality that the cat arrived at
On a sunny roof.
You spurred the ships to set sail from our souls
So we freshened your waters with vast rites
You became our festivity. Your saddlebags
Sagged with coriander seeds and almonds.
Now the world is narrow
And death's mad speed has slackened."

And came the tailors. They did not bring fire and blood.
Yet their sorrows were blood and fire. A tumultuous thing
Express trains were stranded in stations and medications went mad
I roamed the city from one end to the other, not a tick
They dispersed into all the rooms. Tumblers dusty, shoes shriveled up
On the floors bits and clips of fabric,

"scooped up lapels, leftovers of sleeves
shoulder pads, crossed straps and hooks,
buttons and loops
bits of thread, pieces of fabric,
dark evenings and mornings
shop signs and business cards . . ."

all the way up to the groins, there is not even the tiniest death.
A neutral love kept purling over their pallor
They locked up their kitchens and cut out huge horse outfits,

"The horse now dead—they said—
Your gallop once expanded the world.
Your frenzied lunge forward

While we lay down south you galloped on
If any horse was pretty you were prettier
At one bright spot your tail split
The sky into black
and exulted it with your fine embroidered crupper strap.
Your reins made lovely sounds
in your lovely mouth
and everyone shouted for joy.
Your head went so well with our thoughts
and we looked into your eyes with deep respect . . ."

And came the tailors. A standstill was what they wore half-naked and tardy
They were left incomplete. And remained so. They loved their
dusty rooms.
Passing death with sorrow, they worshipped fire.
The city stood at their threshold and they heard its wail
They cut and measured, but neither sewed nor went off
Having put thread through the needles they waited;

"The horse now dead—they said—
That was the loveliest of all, the affinity
between your face and the war
An out-and-out resistance, balance,
and a willful diminution. We knew that.
That tree fed upon our blood
which fed all of us.
Our bafflement before you re-created
a country,
destroyed by trading and the alphabet and leftovers of thread
and the attempt to set everything straight . . ."

Turgut Uyar

Deer Night

Yet nothing in sight inspired fright
Everything was made of nylon that's all
We were dying legion against the sun when we died
But before we found the deer night
We were afraid like little children

You must all know the deer night
In remote jungles green and wild
With the sun's sagging and sinking at the asphalt's edge
It shall redeem all of us from time

While we tilled the soil
We vanished
From gladiators cogwheels strongmen
From giant cities

Concealing it or fighting for it
We rescued the deer night

We were lonely yes but we had hope
To us three houses meant a city
Three pigeons evoked all of Mexico
We cherished our evening strolls on the avenues
And women's yearning for their husbands
Later on we would sip red wine or white wine
Because of the deer night whether we knew it or not

"There are trees beyond the deer night
And the sky where its hoofs touch the water
And chilly moonlight on its forked horns"
Whether you like it or not love is evoked
There were beautiful women and loves in the past
Nowadays too as I know
If you only knew how happy this thought makes me

The loveliest of the deer night of the mountains
I say don't care about anything
Except love and hope
In a single moment three cups and three new songs
The deer night looms in my memory with its downy skin

I know no ship shall give it passage
Nor will neons and theories shed light on its bearings
At Monastery[1] for instance the two of us used to drink
Or make love in bed a man and a woman
Our kisses would get hotter and hotter
Our armpits used to taste more and more luscious
In the darkness of the deer night

It didn't matter much that we were led astray
Just that we recalled what everyone else had forgotten
The silver samovars and the other antiques
We loved not for denial's sake
You might ask was it due to our wickedness
We were neither good nor wicked
If we were different at the beginning and at the end
This was because we were different then

But whatever there was it was in the deer night
If you only knew your palms would perspire with passion
As we gazed night broke out on the pavements
Out of crystal chandeliers and bare female shoulders
We felt strange and incredulous in front of grand hotels
All helplessness was thus all too facile
You'd be wrong to think our sadness was due to great causes
For example three glasses of wine could redeem us
Or stabbing a man
Or spitting in the streets

1. Monastery: A reference to the Balkan town Monastir.

But best of all we would just go away
Into the deer night to sleep

"The eyes of the deer glitter in the night
Fearful and fluttering like fire that sends distress signals
Like sultan's scimitars in the moonlight
On one side of it rocks heaped on rocks
And me on the other side"
But you are pitiful and so am I
No longer consoled by things that have grown old
Domino dots and chilly afternoons
An alien multitude clad in flowery garments
Our shadow curls up at the edge of our feet
Though we might rejoice we know the end
I forget the debts, guarantors, and bonds
The world's lotteries are drawn in my absence
My acquittal is granted at the opening session
I bathe a brunette for myself
I don't dry her hair properly
For myself I drink down a glass of wine
        "Yet the deer night is in the forest
        Sharp blue and rustling
        I enter the deer night"
I recline and kiss myself on both cheeks

Turgut Uyar

Rasp

Like a file rasping such a wind blows
Thorns glow but not the flower
That travesty of an epoch strokes its tarred surface
In its warmth blood freezes it doesn't get lukewarm
True existence straightens up on elbows
The enemy sleeps water doesn't.

Metin Eloğlu

Vanish

I reiterate your face is a laughter
Glance and an armada of life marches into light
A flower that hails from subterranean regions
An eagle gone stark-naked
Now pink is pursued by three persons
Upward along your shoulders
Drive them insane in your hair
Carnation multiple
Carnation shrinking shrunk

Most beauty arises in your most secret places
Lovely as animals suddenly born
Glance and I deliver a poem to the world
A poem is made red round wide
Widest reddest on planes oppressed
A secret is now pursued by three persons
Inward along your eyes
Drive them insane in my lines
Carnation divided
Carnation multiplied multiple

Know your hands in circles of hope
Hands are gazed at holding the void in balance
An extension from hope to man
A plane muddled known only to sight
Love is close while forging day out of night
Now love is chased
By three international persons
Drive them insane in infinity
A tea has many a name
A table many a round

As in ancient days, good day miniatures
Three slaves signing the world sprawled out

Suddenly square suddenly sphinx
A silence where it feels most
A beyond basked in the sunniest sun
Their heads hanging out of the earth
Flowers of vanquished panic perpetuate a history
With inaudible shrieks
In their inmost faces three persons
Drive them insane in Egypt
One man too few
One man along his faith

Hear what the horses hear from the bells
Hear the fires built on the mountains
Awesome age when cities are delved out under us
Ornaments rotten animals ramcrossed
They all compel us to stare
Now a radiance is arrested
By three white-clad persons
Drive them insane in the void
A window too narrow
A window vanishing vanished . . .

Edip Cansever

Bedouin

In the desolate shriveled brown town of my eyes
White-necked camels trudge along behind the weary herdsmen
Who still grope for a meaning day after day
Staring into a place far away
Ask them if they saw at least as much as they see a tale
In the desolate shriveled brown town of my eyes

Toward an unknown place neither day nor death
They just stare
A Bedouin stands among the white thorns
Among gods and suns and fires
Not even a flame nor a plant nor a prayer
In the desolate shriveled brown town of my eyes

Who knows what he seeks perhaps a sating sip of water
Not a stop nor a rest
The white-necked camels could sense nothing even if they came
Even if the weary herdsmen knelt down and crouched before them
As the chilliest desert bird dies once again
In the uniform color of the world

Edip Cansever

Crab

What happens to be uncertain? The place
Left vacant by the dead is filled by nature.
Hoary animal skeletons and fossils have their images
Thrust within extinction
Sometimes the shell of a huge crab.

I know the crabs more than others. There was one
I couldn't forget all these years
It kept going in circles round a rock
As if distilled from petulance or boredom
It seemed to pass again into another boredom
Burying itself in the sand it looked around
I watched it nip its claws with its own sorcery
Since that day I have known the pain and carried it.

Death is sorcery, the ashen mortar of eternity
Where hope is created like savagery
Builders spread their ribs out
Among the yellow broom
Chariots sprout, horses teem
A god arrives barely seen, a god for whatever time
Because death is sorcery
The ashen mortar of eternity.

True, nature is crafty and bewitching
Every day it returns a bit of what it had taken away
It oozes into the cities, houses, wombs
One day I had found myself dead, I was afraid
At this hour of extinction at a desolate spot
I think that's why I have this scar on my neck
It would get covered if I held the mornings out to the sky
With a star left behind from the night
A star the color of ice. And my sleep
Had just ended, what's more

I am getting back
The complex architecture of my dreams
Waves have long remained silent, the sea is spent like silver coins
From bottom to top
From top to bottom
Somehow each beginning has some pain. Morning
First engulfs this pain
And then it ages and goes away.

And the crab sinks its claws right into its belly
Right in the middle. From now on
All you can see is a dead crab embossed
On each silver coin
Only an embossing. Just then
The sky turns hard as rock and hurls a swallow
Chilling the seaweed and the anemone, sunken ships
And the old fishermen in their boats
Rocks, schools of fish, and beacons
Phantom ships come out of their sheaths and multiply
Crew members turn into sculpture, the bazaar
Into windowpanes, plants pasted on mirrors
The moment of suicide has no shadow to be seen
A dead thing casts no shadow
Crabs gush out of excavations one after another
Over columns, arches, mosaics of old
Over mail seals, candelabra, and bowls
Coats of arms, temples, ring stones
And the crab after so much retreat
Again arrives in time for its own death ritual
And death, that daredevil warrior
While etching its fate with its own sorcery
Writes its own one-work history too.

Clearly the crab has found a way out
Not through the sand, a way out of itself
Clearly the crab has found a way out

Yet, because the wind is ahead of the ashes
Because intuition comes before death
Human beings sense these redundant swimmers
Stirring between two skies
Even if there is no self-recognition like someone else's dream.

A three-way conversation is different, to a solitary person
One opens up
Hope is created there even if it's like savagery
And the heart turns into a swift-stinging pointer
While containing its life
It works up its own death.

Edip Cansever

The Desolate Locust

"This locust is lame," you said
with no dread or pity in your voice.

Bird and beast felt no longing for turmoil or peace.
We were looking for a four-leaf clover.

Like the head of a statue buried through the ages
now emerging slowly
from among the grass
timid but proud

A locust
stood against a scarlet cloud
a godly shadow.

"When the almond tree blooms,
and the locust grows sluggish
and the caper berry is without effect,
Because man goes to his lasting home
and mourners go about the street . . ."[1]

"Shall we catch it? It can't get away."

The holy book echoes in its deafness:
"The wind's tooth, the rain's demon . . ."

"Can it see?"
Neither of us knew.
Standing there, it stared at us
A dwarfish god fallen apart from the swarm,

1. The quotations in italics are from the Bible, the Caliph Umar, early Arabic verse, and Southey's *Thabala.*

More ancient than the sun,
more parched than the simoon . . .

Neither bewildered
nor furious
nor a rebel,
A sage hiding his own blindness,
it steals the glitter of our eyes.

Its wings carry the sun's hunger and hell's downpour,
Taut,
Poised to leap:
"The epic of the locust
always ends with an elegy."

"mares waiting to plunge into the battle lines
their heads crowned with a gold wreath
their faces human . . ."
Each locust weighing as much as its own hunger
not crushed under the shepherd's feet
it listens to the hymns chanted in temples
strangled over the rainbow and in caves
Its blood,
beyond the terror of the pharaohs,
about to trickle, longing for a new age.

"We are the army of God
We produce ninety-nine eggs.
If the hundredth were complete
We would consume the whole world
And all that is in it."

Is the eye of the hurricane
afraid of the ferns now?
If a lizard has pangs of hunger
one morsel, one awn . . .

"The ancients thought burning the few locusts
Kept the swarms from coming."
Damnation's footprints crack open the domes.
One flame is not enough.
Build giant fires.

Panting with despair, stallions broke loose
"They were carrying death
They covered the face of the whole earth
so that the land was darkened
and they did eat every herb of the land
and all the fruit of the trees
and there remained no green thing in the trees
or in the herbs of the fields . . ."

"This locust is all alone."
Freer than any soul on a blazing doomsday,
A single leg to cross the Sahara.

You whispered: "Let's not scare it."
Your voice became immaculate milk for a moment.

We held back our steps
and yet the swarm had lunged with a giant appetite.

Wingless fairies tottering in the midst of a gentle song
are now a jungle . . .

And vengeance, that genius going mad,
casts a shadow over the sun.

Soil and water
Are blood brothers
The tumult of the judgment day
And a brigade of midget heroes.

This punishment is—for what crime?

The ears of corn, like a vanquished army,
Waited for a tyrant to put them to the sword.

Blackberries are shivering in the promised land
We nailed new amulets to old idols
Each crucifix has a mirage now

"The Angel of the Apocalypse
opened the bottomless pit
and there arose a smoke out of it
as the smoke of a great furnace
and they burst out of the earth
stronger like scorpions

they had received orders
not to destroy
the grass and the trees

they were to devastate
only those who bear on their brows
no faith in God"

From a blind horizon to the darkest horizons
The spikes that God adores have fallen victim.

Heaven has forgotten love.

"Every green thing was eaten up;
not even the bitter bark of the orange
and the pomegranate escaping. A most
dreadful famine ensued. The poor were
seen to wander over the country, deriving
a miserable subsistence from the roots of
plants, and women and children followed
the camels from whose dung they picked

the undigested grains of barley . . . the roads and streets exhibited the unburied carcasses of the dead . . . fathers sold their children and husbands their wives."

An old shepherd looked for an antidote
To uproot the curse:

In the ditches he dug with prayers
He's now madly beating the locust water.

"I heard locusts are born of animal carcasses."

Lions and rhinoceroses shall be buried
And the insatiable worms shall become immortal.

"Look, it's as if it's smiling."

Merciless skies will soon empty themselves out:
The earth is writhing like a leper.

It's been ages since the prophets turned silent:
The locust is the Messiah waiting in the womb.

The cross on its brow
is about to split open . . .

a dash of wisdom a gnarled angel
how many nations
both enslaved and hungry . . .

"If you refuse to let my people go,
I warn you, the east wind shall blow tomorrow
and fill your country with locusts."

In the season of tyrants earth and sky shrivel up
like the breasts of the mothers whose milk has turned black.

"Locusts, they have no king
yet they migrate all in array."

In a dungeon far away there is an invincible voice,
Is it tearful or raging, no one knows?

And they broke out and pounced like a juggernaut of eagles
mother earth who has known all calamities
witnessed a bloodless massacre
weeds covered in the sea and vultures in the sky

friend and foe heard the tumult of the demons of Hell

"God has created a thousand nations of
creatures . . . and the first one to perish
among them will be the locusts which,
when they perish, will be followed by
other nations like a string of pearls
when that string is cut."

"How do locusts make love?"
suddenly the quiver of love in the pink wells . . .
two branches touched each other in fondness.

A godly voice stirred
with fury and compassion:

"I will restore to you
the years that the locust hath eaten."

We lay
on the sparkling grass
And made love

hoping to turn survival into a volcano
The two of us naked in this desolate silence
                        a sprouting love

In its devouring dreams
                        Doesn't this locust see it all?

"Maybe," you said, "it isn't lame?"

Talat S. Halman

Blood Lurks Under All Words

Speak to me of mail wagons
Blood lurks under all words
Speak to me of Aesop's accursed tongue
Blood lurks under all words
This might turn out to be an unexpected day
The lion might recline on rock beds like a brother
Order a cup of tea in the rain's fragrance
Blood lurks under all words
As you stood there suddenly
Your voice unfurled like a fan
On autumn's most tumultuous wing
And on the sky's thinnest branch

Blood lurks under all words
This might well be an unexpected day
Saturday might flow like a fountain
The unvoiced consonants in its shriek
Are last night's weight in your veins
How wonderful is the way peddlers speak
How crowded they are in their felt hats
And the teats of girls who sell flowers
Are less guilty than swallows' eggs
Blood lurks under all words
There's no tree here that will shed its leaves
But sunbeams could shed all their colors
Your memory is on the job all the time
Among poets who will bear witness
Among friendly actors

The journey could search for a rhyme
In the knot on the horse's tail

Death could search for a rhyme
On its white shirt

The road looks for a rhyme and finds it
In the similarity of the road bends

Blood lurks under all words
For instance take a rose in your hand
Blood lurks under all words
Hold it before a mirror for five minutes
Blood lurks under all words
Then take a little slice of that mirror
In white gauze
And put it into your vest pocket
That mirror smells of a whole lifetime
Blood lurks under all words
That blood is your smile
It has seeped into life's depths
It is black there it is red
It skips from branch to branch
It loves the stories told to children
But when it comes to the matter of defense
It defends only the flame
And the sun's unfading kernel
On desolate mountaintops

This could turn out to be an unexpected day
Blood lurks under all words

Cemal Süreya

Just at These Hours

Just at these hours the water bleeds like a fresh wound
At the ends of streets, at their tiny tips.
Your eyes—the cistern of the sun—
Are like an object that should not be in a house
Mourning the dead, like a shattered mirror
At these hours.
Here we watch a man carrying a ladder
Like Christ who is never seen without his crucifix
We see a man carrying twelve steps on his back
I love him so much, and this bird too
You share this love; anyway, when you love
You weed out the whole earth
As the trellises hanging over the mouths of buildings
Go way beyond their own boundaries,
Dogs bark up a secret mountain.

These are good I say these know all about you
Or else how could the fish
That live on the border of carbon
Know of the day of exodus leaking out of the bucket
How could the Muslims enamored of miracles
Hang their overcoats on the Prophet's fingers
And enter God's house?
And how could the mountain roads
Near which the Greeks copulated with goats
During the Return of the Ten Thousand be decked out?

And yet and yet each word we use
While making love
Is the furniture knocked over by a burglar.

Streets turned violet with the minibuses
Where they trade wheat for money
Trade money for bread

Trade bread for tobacco
Trade tobacco for suffering
And where suffering isn't bartered for anything any more.
In those streets.
The clocks show the rain,
Today, this tiny Tuesday
Istanbul lacks everything except its hills,
Only Galata[1]
Galata
Slowly feeds to the sea
Its inexhaustible passion for rusting
That it nurtured in the night's basements
In the form of a harmonica
Our roots flinch from their own flowers

Cemal Süreya

1. Galata: A district of the city of Istanbul.

Monument of the Unknown Student

Look here, underneath this black marble
Is buried a child who would have come
    to the blackboard
From nature if he had one more breath of life
He was killed in the class on Government

The wrong question posed by both government and
    nature was:
"Where does Transoxiana run into?"
The only correct answer from a hand raised in the
    last row was:
"Into the heart of the rebellion of pale
    lower-class children."

To suppress this death, too, his old father,
    secondhand peddler,
Who tied around his neck a purple embroidered
    kerchief, wrote:
I mean I had convinced him that he had his toys.
Since that day his mother, washerwoman at night,
    who wears
A soldier's greatcoat and secretly suckles the foal
    of deer, dictated:
Oh they put my son's hard work in his hands.

His friends wove this poem out of oleanders:
Don't worry, No. 1281 at the tuition-free NCO
    school of suicide,
In every child's heart there is an older child
On children's holidays the whole class will send you
    birds not tucked into envelopes.

Ece Ayhan

Kindertotenlieder

In the streets
deadly oranges
and
indigo clouds
whatever
the hour
a ship with a cargo of sadness
in the Mediterranean
deadly
indigo
oranges and clouds

Her linen dress
immaculate
smelling of soap
not properly rinsed
the same fruitful girl
smokes tobacco and chokes
in a giant's arms tattooed in five colors

Whatever
the hour
the death songs of children
whatever
the hour
sprout from the open window
out of the ashen house

Ece Ayhan

The Voice of Poetry by the Seashore

To me a star without a country that longs for one
Is poetry tossed into the sea

A half-moon slashed by palaces that will burn up
Its death left to the voice of poetry by the seashore.

Ece Ayhan

Rain

Rain, rain, what does this explain?

So many drenched sparrows in all this fog
Have held and lifted sorrow from one end.

Rain, rain, what does this explain?
The final summer is folded, last flames are out
The last fugitive, last brigand to swoop down the highway
Have held and lifted sorrow from one end.

Rain, rain, what does this explain?
The play ends, those sharp lines of autumn
Love which has been roughed up by death too
Have held and lifted sorrow from one end.

Gülten Akın

All Men Die

Because the skies grow white with boredom
the wind wrinkles and the leaf falls
and in the midst of a withered blue
the gulls escape and the crimson deer.
There, see the gold and black currents
mothers, lost souvenir picture,
poverty, that frightful woman.
Quiet, it's the day for all remembrance,
black rain and the rainbow
Slowly gently all men die.

Human voices should cease
For trucks may fall off the mountain road.
A silver watch in hock at the pawnbroker
and the suitcase forgotten at the checkroom
are meteors that come to pass
through the air and the blue celluloid.
Loneliness with its defective marble
is a sacred prey offered to God,
then it turns into the luster of ruby.

Because the skies grow white with blood
a vein throbbing and out of breath
in the heart of the petulant sea
and in the pulse of the soil,
bloodstream is like being forgotten.
The gallows and the cross and the flower
shiver in the same wind,
the whisper of the bed should cease,
the amber glittering in the hand:
with bread shackled and heads bowed,
the men of those women pass by.
And the sad delta of brief lives
an album, a song, a child.

The ruby of some frozen sorrow
as pale as the scratch pads of kids
sparkles over the battlefields,
all the groves are the moonlight,
loves are the fulcrum you cannot reach,
the dirge that slashes and makes the hands bleed.
Oblivion is what lingers in the mind,
Leaping, defeated, dying deer
pen and pencil from which agony never strays.
Men are a brief word,
Non pasarán in Spain,
church bells turning red
a long shadow over the cathedrals
Mamma mia in Italy
the rocks where the palms feel and hear the world,
In Mexico a drooping mustache *Viva.*
Rivers dry up, love keeps quiet
and men are the harshest word
in barren squalid Anatolia.

Men are big and defeated,
an adventurous boy will heed no one
a sick man who mumbles in the splash of water
and a mad lover until daybreak
inventive, terrible, and ashamed.
Useless are all the lilac trees,
men can never understand
the sadness of children born and dead,
for they die beforehand.

Because the skies grow white with blood,
there are always vanquished stars,
the diary, the sundial, and the battlefield,
a face
are all that blood.

Crystal spreads its sparkle,
deathlessness, that intractable tomb,
moonlight makes the sea endure and itself,
while all things pass on and go forth,
slowly gently all men die.

Ahmet Oktay

All the King's Men

you were a king how can I help recall
who could not find a place to put his hands
except the sagging shoulders of his subjects
you were the king this was certainly your right

the sea was yours the sea of plunges and hugs
when the moon stood on one side of the night
and while hairs almost reached the other hairs
yours was the night of sleeping side by side

blood is more valiant than all we have known
you reached it as if your hands had put it there
how can I help recall you were the king
your men poured out of the city's fountains

Kemal Özer

Like a Flame

The poet's wife is like a flame.
Wherever he goes he comes face to face with her;
in the mirror she holds, the poet sees
the first clues that will turn into poems in the future.

The poet's wife is like a flame.
The way her eyebrows almost touch each other
but aren't linked together,
the way her hair is bound for the shoulders
and yet stops short on the back of the neck
keep reminding the poet
of how he gets dizzy when he stares
from the edge of a precipice.

He educated his heart with the lines he read
in the always open book of her eyes;
he learned from her transforming hands
to hold fast until he got results
whenever he undertook a task.

A gift. A flame that sunny days
cannot cause to fade and even the most invincible storm
cannot extinguish.

A small flame. Sensitive and trembling.

Kemal Özer

The Tuft

his eyes are asleep spread on the table
the child scans the map
scared on the verge of throwing up
unless he holds his mother's nearest hand

they died their lines were drawn how can he know
they died turning a cold shoulder to death
their lines drawn the girls and ardahan[1]
when their eyes disappear from sleeping and weeping

it is blood which just passed it's so white
stones and covers are all so white
it is blood which passed through the gleaming street
it's smeared all over the children's hands

every child is the clock tower of a town
in which aerialists swing toward death
the terrible tower of the death hours
one foot toward his mother the other toward death.

Kemal Özer

1. Ardahan: A town in easternmost Turkey.

now for whatever reason

now, for whatever reason, everything
tastes like the butterfly that disintegrates

silence, as you know
is the best-tended garden
smiles are now in exile there
pains are brothers
yet no one understands that

be it in love or in spring-deaths
all rivers give way
to engrave itself the rose
needs no apprentice or master

forgive me, children!
dip my words in the peevish salt of gray doves
then look:
has there ever been a guide worse than sorrow?

there's been none so far

but now, whatever the reason, everything
tastes like the butterfly that disintegrates

Hilmi Yavuz

In Praise of My Father

I praise and exalt my father
who never left me fatherless
because he gave himself a long life.

They killed him every day
sometimes at a clerk's desk
sometimes at the grocer or the café
they killed my father every day.

My father is a set of dead fathers
getting smaller and smaller in the mirror
getting bigger and bigger in the mirror;
they claimed he trampled the sun
that he failed to see the shadow
because he said "no"
or didn't say "yes" at appropriate moments
they kept killing my father.

My father lived by dying
dying he lived long
I'm a dying son too
I praise and exalt my father.

Hydra
2 August 1981

Özdemir İnce

Our Sons

They see the backs of our sons;
we look into their eyes which are ours.

—My son, my wounded branch!

We know our sons by the sound of their footsteps,
by their smell in the midst of countless weeds;
they smell of tobacco, fresh sweat, and green grass.

—My son, my wounded breath!

Our sons are the torrent of spring in April and May,
sometimes an eclipse, sometimes the longest day.

—My son, my wounded waters!

The weary faces of fathers on their faces,
the sad fury of mothers on their faces;
and on their foreheads love's ineradicable seal.

—My son, my wounded father!

Hearts cringe at dawn when the prayer call is chanted
the crystal mirror of inmost lives lies shattered;
the soul is in the dragon's mouth behind the seven hills.

—My son, my wounded constellation!

They see the backs of our sons;
we stare into their eyes that are now a prison grille.

—My son, my wounded God!

Ankara
17 June 1981

Özdemir İnce

From: Lecture Notes

45

When I was twenty,
I used to say I should be like Sartre
or nothing.

Now I am forty.
I haven't turned out to be like Sartre.
I have become like myself.
I still have respect for Sartre if not admiration
But today I know my capabilities well.
With each passing day, I try to be
even more like myself.

49

I have no burning ambition to last into the future.
All I want is to strike roots into my own day.

51

I am not in search of a miracle
I am trying to create a miracle.

68

"A dungeon for dreams and ideas!"
That must be
the biggest dream and idea of the tyrants.

80

In ancient Greece and Rome
lovemaking
was an ordinary matter
that required no special attention.

The poisoning of Eros
has been the work of monotheistic religions.

101

One day I saw
how much a person can age in one day.

Ferit Edgü

The Dagger

Back in the fall we had buried our dagger
In this courtyard covered with square tiles.
That dagger was both precious and sharp.
Its handle must have melted away by now
Looking like the mossy hair of the herdsmen.

The blood of worms and hawks must be clinging
Onto its skeleton lying in the ground.
Spilling all over the blood-tiles of the yard
The blood of the hawks that sent their flight
Deep down in the form of a disheveled line.

The sea has lit the lamps on its streets.
The dagger received its only defeat from us.
Out of the country of its spout it gazes at night,
At birds that cling to their wings as they fall.
We received our final defeat from the dagger.

For some reason it frightens the gray silence
Of a beggar's voice and the mountaineers' sky,
It frightens the faces of rope-hearted seamen
Who cross the seas each with a panther on his back:
That noise which the dagger makes while rusting.

Ülkü Tamer

Sunday in the Meadows

They put up a little windmill
not far from the gallows.
The windmill turns as the brigand gasps,
the blood swelling in his lungs
blends into the brush
held by grandpa the painter
who is looking for a nice shade of red
to paint the windmill.

Just then the beavers run away.

Ülkü Tamer

Responses for Poetry

1

Poetry is the night's brother
and the day's mother.

It is the grandfather in the heart.

2

Poetry is the spider's voice,
the wall's song.

It is the folk song of the mason.

3

Poetry is the rain's valley,
the sweat at the roots of the hair.

It is the fresh flag of the vessels.

4

Poetry is the frame for posters,
the line of the letters in the alphabet.

It is the metal inside the bell.

5

Poetry is the blue of the smaller trucks,
the heroism of the big trucks.

It is the unwritten history of the phaetons.

6

Poetry is the drinking bucket's fountain,
the well's traveler.

It is the guard at the source.

7

Poetry is the acrobats' balance,
the jugglers' spectator.

It is the magicians' dream.

8

Poetry is the grape's sun,
the apple's worm.

It is the powder of bramble.

9

Poetry is the symbol of silver,
steel construction.

It is the bullet's lunge forward.

10

Poetry is the thornbush of the fence,
the plowing of the field.

It is the farmhand's absentmindedness.

11

Poetry is the sand fly's hour,
the glowworm's second.

It is the years of nature.

12

Poetry is death's shadow,
the cover on living.

It is the child's defense.

13

Poetry is the sieve on the beach,
the boulder's dregs.

It is the vein offered by marble.

14

Poetry is the mattress of insomnia,
the map of sleep.

It is the awakening of the balcony.

15

Poetry is fire's messenger,
the arsonist.

It is the bird perched on the volcano.

Ülkü Tamer

Unexpected Sights

I

Cruising downhill gaining speed all the time
An idle hearse on which coffins are lined up
Dragged by a dreamy chestnut mare
It was carrying dead youths out of the city
And now a fearful scurrying along the way
Faces on the windowpanes trembling with fright
It hurtles downhill like a scream
And from the coffins that keep falling off
Windowpanes crashing all over the streets
Are scattered toys and forgotten wild flowers

II

The shore was calm with motionless bodies
The sky unfurled with an unexpected light
A boredom grew along faces out of the void
Woven by the summer sky
First he saw a child making sand castles
Approached the shore like a mysterious vessel
A corpse smiling on a translucent glacier
Judging by his hands he must have been a stoker
On liners that cruise the summer seas
In whose dreams cool waters flow on

Turgay Gönenç

Toward Freedom

I am left behind steeped in all this calamity
My discretion is dead my body's edifice is gone

My chest is girded by a thin taut steel band
Which presses my flesh all the way down

My lilacs screech and the walls weep and cry
Symmetrical arts could burst they are so thirsty

The child collapses and hearts perch on hearts
They tear my pulse out in it throbs a father's vein

A defeat that sent generations into a frenzy now sinks
My mind is pitch-black and my heart a white dot

Flow of fate all my deeds and gains get an applause
A wayward discovery waves go on and on swelling

There's no other way I shall shout loud and clear or else
This wretched ship with its cargo of riot on the heart's rocks

War. It's not for my downtrodden flesh or my cursed dog's life
The way I kill as I must beautifully moderately without torment

War is imminent brother have you been sharpened real well
Your swords and your dagger take up thousands of volumes

I believe in you believe in we believe in[1]
In *"la ilahe illallah la ilahe illallah"*[2]

1. This line appears in English in the original.
2. "There is no god but God" (Islamic affirmation in Arabic).

Rise now you're lofty do the ritual wash don the flowing waters
Your face and arms will not build the fire your head and thin feet

The world is a roadside mansion and a guest immortal in life
Abused as it is passed and the guest undressed to lust when he is kissed

Not the stable of lust but the earth
Not a pig-sty but the ground and the soil

The soil you find in between my two glances
Four-cornered walls black covers and the sounds of migration

I am closing accept it command it
Wrap me more in covers with a thousand angles

I wish I could stand at your threshold
For a thousand years for a thousand more

To raise one curtain out of myriad curtains
My head flushes my face blushes I'm humble I know my limits

An arrival that quietly sheds the spears of my body
Let it come my chest can take in no more than a few trees

Let my quiet and even more quiet spears drop
Entrusted today to a dog that leaps forward suddenly and barks

A thousand exhaustions and redemption and Godly greetings in entering the meadow
Kneel like a mountain be a river to yourself hold the thunderbolts hold and drop them

There is no quiet or even more quiet stirring in your glance
Let your tears turn into a lake in the ground

You were a sort of rebellion your cure was a weeping heart
Make way. You now pass through so many places of seclusion

Now I am beckoned to that beautiful love beseeching me
I stop and stand so many deaths the mounts on my shoulders

This meadow must be paradise a heavenly rank numbering us
This pit must be fire a phalanx of fire numbering us

How about this road? This one that the feet walk unaware of their body
And the body attached to the feet facing the feet becoming feet

Know your heart unto the heights

Tell it just the way a mountain tells it
Begin just the way a mountain moans

Poet you too took the path of your ancestors
I fear your weight cannot carry these countless calamities

Cahit Zarifoğlu

Some Day for Sure

Today first I made love, then I joined the march
I am tired, spring is here, this summer I must learn how to fire a gun
Books are accumulating, my hair is growing long, there's a tumultuous
rush everywhere
I am still young, I want to see the world, kissing is wonderful,
thinking is lovely, one day we shall overcome!
Some day we shall triumph for sure, I tell you, loan sharks of
old! You geese! You grand vizier!
My darling is barely eighteen, we stroll on the boulevard, eat
sandwiches and talk about the world
Flowers bloom all the time and wars go on, how can everything end
with one bomb, how can those filthy men win
I keep thinking, I splash water on my face, I put on a clean shirt
One day this oppression will end, this feast for thieves will end
But I am tired now, I keep smoking, I'm wearing a dirty raincoat
Smoke rises to the sky from the central heating system, there
are Vietnamese books in my pocket
I'm thinking of my friends at the other end of the world, of the
rivers at the other end
Quietly a girl dies there, she dies quietly
I go over the bridges, on a dark rainy day, I walk to the station
These houses sadden me, this ramshackle world
People and the roar of motors, the fog, the flowing water
What can I do . . . What should I do . . . There are dregs of sadness
everywhere
I lean my forehead against an iron grille, those old days come to mind
I too was a child, naturally I was going to have my own loves
I think of coming back from the movies, and of my mother, how
can everything die, how can a person be forgotten
Oh sky! I used to lie underneath you, oh glittering fields
What can I do . . . What should I do . . . Later I read Descartes
My stubble gets longer, I love this girl, a short walk to Çankaya[1]

1. Çankaya: A fashionable section of Ankara.

Sunday, a sunny Sunday, my heart surges as I mix with people
A child stares out of the window, an exquisite child with huge dreamy eyes
Then his brother who resembles Lermontov's childhood photos looks out
I am writing a poem on the typewriter, I'm wondering about the
newspapers, suddenly I hear the chirping of birds
I am a humble poet, my love, everything excites me
After all what is there to cry about when I catch sight of a common
ordinary man
Looking at the man's ears, neck, eyes, eyebrows, and the twitches on his
face
I say "The people, yes," I say "Oh child," then I burst into tears
Then I put the curse on all individualistic poets and head for
the fruit market to buy oranges
I put the curse on those effusions of words, withered hearts, man's
salvation, etc.
I put the curse on those bookworms, then I pardon them
I wonder how things turn out after long winter nights
All the things told in tales after those long winter nights
From time to time I pause to think about these, a sadness comes in the
wake of a joy
My heart is a spring sky with all its fiddle-faddle. In short a heart in the
Turkish language
Waiting is so wearying, here and there I talk about a lot of things in a mad
rush
I take a bus, I scrutinize an insect holding it by its wings
In the past I used to walk in springtime to regions where there were ruins
and meadows
Reminded of that old American's poem, that poem about autumn
There were meadows in the poem, reminiscent of spring to be sure
This way I get ready for a new passion, for dashing out into the streets
again
To throw myself headlong off a precipice
The image of something big and blue lingers in my mind, it's
probably from a film I have seen
A hat, a sky in a flurry, a warm spurious world
I keep talking and telling stories, but there is no end to my homesickness

I can squander all my loves in a split second, I am reminded of those rain-
drenched roads
Smell of gasoline, damp poles, my father is fat and warm like a loaf of
bread
I used to sleep. Suddenly you notice there's a new feature film at
the movie theater, a new girl in town, a new waiter at the
café.
She stood on the balcony sad, dressed in her robe . . .
Now why should this sadden me, why is this heartrending, why all this
dithering
As if I am going to die tomorrow or the police will storm in soon
To impound my books, my typewriter, this poem, my darling's photo
hanging on the wall
To ask what's your father's name, where were you born, would
you kindly come to the precinct
I'm thinking of my friends at the other end of the world, of the rivers at
the other end
Quietly a girl dies there, she's dying quietly in Vietnam
Weeping I draw the picture of a heart in the air
I wake crying, one day we shall defeat them for sure!
Some day we shall triumph, I tell you, importers, exporters,
I tell you, Islam's Chief Dignitary!
We shall overcome for sure! One day we shall emerge victorious!
We are going to repeat this a thousand times!
Then we shall multiply it a thousand times and then a thousand times
again with anthems
I and my darling and my friends shall march in the boulevards
We shall march with the gushing joy of being created anew
We shall march, increasing and multiplying as we go . . .

Ataol Behramoğlu

To Stay Out of the Fight

You have to let go of the rope in the end
And leave this horse somewhere . . .
Out there, the fight spreads at full speed
You must let go of the rope
Like a brook running loose—
Again one must give up living.

It is the bewilderment of untested weapons
That repel my hands this way,
Beyond the hills the hoofbeats of a horse
March into my expanding veins
Gently in the warmth of my hands
Out there, the fight spreads at full speed.

The hoofbeats of a horse in my veins
(The fight spreads—
Quit all these fights, just love me,
Love life, carefree, unbridled . . .)
The hoofbeats of a horse in my veins
At the outset a fight is like the first day of love:
Our bodies are strangers to ourselves.

Sennur Sezer

A Shroud for My Darling

The shrine of a woman whose hair blazes in henna
soars overhead in an undertone
these violet autumn days inflict their madness
driving you out of your senses and books
tumors, dead ants
chills and shivers cover me
curiosity
is the genesis of a revolutionary
and above me in an undertone fly
cancer, begonia, death.

White gauze behind the windowpane
and eyes plucked out
real human eyes heavy like rocks
a mother who endures all the agony
and the dust stirred up by her corpse,
you warden of anguish, you autumn days.

Under the rain of the rebel leader
I clobber my own scorched and paltry beauty
Saturday afternoons pierce like a cramp
my hope
is a ferocious animal
which keeps toppling the banknotes and mass meetings
and chokes the houses we live in
with the aroma of cinnamon and with weariness,
curiosity
is the genesis of a revolutionary
in the bazaars some coppersmiths wash
and women who knead dough are dragged with clangs
in their mortars they pound their stubborn streak
and their vile hopes too.

I cannot love a girl secretly
a thousand curiosities prick me all over
those gloomy smells of incense, our mothers
craving food in pregnancy must eat dirt
untie the ropes of my heart against the moon
my heavenly pain throbs in my wrists
sawdust convulsing sawdust
sawdust of the sledge that beats on my temples.

İsmet Özel

Lot's Woman

;further.

I

I open my bag: A few dice,
a pouch of powdered gold leaf, a long
sad dream I kept out of everyone's reach,
forgotten words from my language, unforgettable
voices, an adverse prosody. I am tired
my friend: I come from the depths of history
and of the globe, I passed so many times through
streams and night deserts: I never lost my way:
ever since I left my city I could never
find it. Although I'm not hungry,
I'm not full of desire or passion: The moment
I'm waiting for hasn't arrived, as if my darling
whose love I can never have enough of isn't born yet
I came and I'm leaving now: I've arrived and shall arrive.

II

"Behind her," it is written
"he looked back, and a pillar of salt emerged."
I never saw it. From behind her
I gouged my eyes with my own hands,
and never saw what she had seen. Then,
I cut off both my hands, the first time
I came to a halt after crossing thousands
of acres of land: Since that day I held neither
plow nor pencil: What's someone else's hand, I didn't
touch one. I was, shall I be: I've aged, I've had
my fill. *If the sky is brass and the earth is iron*
as they'd read it to me: The time left to me is no more
than spring showers, I am going near my woman
who gave her life for a single glance.

Enis Batur

Last Swans

the swans too are bound to darken
if death is narration
some day our bourgeois necks will lose
their passion for stout ropes anyway
    (I put on the blankest of papers
    the eternal black of marble
    and a hand severed at dawn that unfurls the world
    conforming to the rules of the night
    and to the daytime barricades)
the real cheap collateral of our selves
endows all this weeping of ours with no power
which means the flowers of theft in our bleeding hands
and maybe this is why the poems of murder
    should be loved dearly
if every creative act is a bright suicide
    (our hands
    our obsessed
    foster hands
    you are bloody slabs of marble that grow when cut off
    solitude resembles wolves
    and if what we create is the longest weeping
    my hands
    my terrifying hands
    you are mine
    or whatever is left of me . . .)
in the name of the sense of suicide
living the adventure of the collapse of the bourgeois class

Murathan Mungan

Waiting Beside a Friend's Coffin

Waiting beside a friend's coffin
I was afraid of catching your eyes,
Of seeing the painful trembling of your lips
Which I had kissed in some room only yesterday.

I felt guilty, waiting erect
Beside the deceased
One by one my friends are dead and gone
Leaving behind them an age of grief.

Yesterday I gave you a rose, you were happy
Now I put a rose on this coffin
Side by side, strange and absurd
They flapped their wings and flew away.

Waiting beside a friend's coffin
You and I sat through the whole night
Recalling what our generation lived through
One by one, a child plucked
        all the roses in us.

Ahmet Erhan

Biograpical Notes

•

About the Editors

•

Acknowledgments

Biographical Notes

GÜLTEN AKIN (1933–), who holds a law degree from Ankara University, is generally recognized as Turkey's leading woman poet. In addition to numerous collections of poems, most of which are notable for their tender lyricism as well as social protest, she has published plays, collections of essays, and dictionaries. She has been extensively translated into foreign languages. Her major awards include Varlık, Turkish Language Society, and Sedat Simavi.

SABAHATTİN KUDRET AKSAL (1920–1993) achieved prominence as poet and playwright. He received a graduate degree in philosophy from the University of Istanbul. After teaching philosophy at several high schools, he held a variety of jobs including director of the City Conservatory of Istanbul and artistic director of the City Opera. Later he taught aesthetics and psychology at the City Conservatory and the Academy of Fine Arts. He won many of Turkey's top awards for his collections of short stories, plays, and poetry.

MELİH CEVDET ANDAY (1915–2002) was a towering figure of Turkish literature. A prolific writer, he achieved renown not only as a poet but also as novelist, playwright, essayist, columnist, and translator. His works were translated into numerous major and minor languages. He received many of Turkey's most prestigious awards for his poetry, plays, and translations.

ÖZDEMİR ASAF (1923–1981) attracted attention with his aphorisms and epigrammatic poems in the 1960s and 1970s. Some of his translations are also quite popular.

ECE AYHAN (1931–2002) was one of the uniquely original modern poets of Turkey. Virtually all of his collections of poems are notable for their obscurantism. He was a graduate of the Faculty of Political Science at Ankara University and worked for some years as a provincial administrator. In addition to his poetry, Ayhan published collections of essays and memoirs.

ENİS BATUR (1952–) studied humanities at the Middle East Technical University in Ankara and literature and philosophy in Paris. He has been a highly successful publisher and editor of cultural and literary periodicals. Since 1988 he served for fifteen years as director of publications at a leading publishing house, Yapı Kredi Yayıncılık. Batur has published a prodigious number of books of poetry, essays, criticism, and translations. His books have been translated into many languages, including Italian, Persian, and Flemish.

ATAOL BEHRAMOĞLU (1942–) is one of the most versatile writers of his generation. In addition to many collections of poems, he has published major anthologies, a play, a children's book, numerous collections of essays, and translations. He holds a degree in Russian language and literature and currently teaches Russian Literature at the University of Istanbul. In the 1970s and 1980s he lived abroad, mainly in Moscow and Paris, where he studied comparative poetics at the Sorbonne. Since the 1990s he has also written a column for the influential Istanbul daily *Cumhuriyet.*

İLHAN BERK (1918–). A prolific and highly influential poet, Berk has been a remarkable innovator for decades. Since 1935 he has published dozens of poetry books, anthologies, and translations. He has won virtually all of Turkey's major literary awards.

SALÂH BİRSEL (1919–1999) was one of the most whimsical of modern Turkish poets and essayists. He graduated from the Department of Philosophy at the University of Istanbul; later he worked as a teacher of French and as a public servant. He served many years as the editor in chief of the journal and other publications of the Turkish Language Society. He is also famous for his multivolume memoirs and his numerous translations of novels and plays from the French.

EDİP CANSEVER (1928–1986). A protagonist of the movement of the 1950s and 1960s dubbed the "Second New," he introduced formal innovations, a brave new style, and philosophical concerns in his poetry.

NECATİ CUMALI (1921–2001) was one of the most versatile of the major modern Turkish writers—poet, playwright, novelist, essayist, and translator. A graduate of the Faculty of Law, Ankara University, he practiced law for seven years, following which he worked at the Turkish Press Attaché's office in Paris and as an editor at Radio Istanbul. Later, he spent a few years in Tel Aviv. He devoted his last three decades exclusively to writing.

ASAF HALET ÇELEBİ (1907–1958) was a remarkable avant-garde poet who stood among the pioneers of free verse and experimented with surrealism. His interest in mythology and mysticism prompted him to forge a synthesis of East and West in his verse. He was a major translator of Rumi, Khayyam, and Indian literature.

FAZIL HÜSNÜ DAĞLARCA (1914–) stands as a towering figure of modern Turkish poetry, who has published more than a hundred collections. With the exception of Nazım Hikmet, he has been translated into more languages than any other modern Turkish poet. He exclusively writes poetry and remains unique in the sense that his poetry bears the influence of no Turkish or non-Turkish poet. In addition to all of Turkey's major prizes, Dağlarca received the prize of the International Poetry Forum (Pittsburgh) and was the "Poet of the Year" at the Struga Poetry Evenings and the Rotterdam Poetry Festival.

AHMET MUHİP DIRANAS (1908–1980) was one of Turkey's most beloved lyric poets and a prominent playwright. His poetry is notable for its formal excellence and neo-romantic sensibilities.

FERİT EDGÜ (1936–) is a foremost poet, fiction writer, and essayist who has won some of Turkey's prestigious awards. After studying at Istanbul's Academy of Fine Arts, he went to Germany and then to Paris where he studied for six years at the Académie Feu, the Sorbonne, and the Louvre. He is also well known for his collections of essays.

METİN ELOĞLU (1927–1985). An avant-garde poet, Eloğlu published numerous volumes. He was also a painter.

AHMET ERHAN (1958–) is an award-winning poet who has published many collections. He holds a graduate degree in Turkish language and literature.

NÜZHET ERMAN (1926–1996). With degrees from the Faculty of Political Science and the Faculty of Law at Ankara University, Erman served in various high-level bureaucratic posts including governor of five administrative provinces. His poems are collected in several volumes.

BEDRİ RAHMİ EYUBOĞLU (1913–1975) was one of Turkey's most successful painters in addition to being a widely popular poet and essayist. After studying at Istanbul's Academy of Fine Arts, he studied painting in France for two years. He was for many years a professor of painting at the Academy of Fine Arts.

TURGAY GÖNENÇ (1939–) is a graduate of the Faculty of Political Science at Ankara University. He worked some years at the State Statistical Institute and taught at the Aegean and Ninth of September Universities in Izmir. Gönenç is also a painter.

TALAT S. HALMAN. *See* pp. 187–88.

NAZIM HİKMET (1902–1963) is Turkey's internationally famous poet who introduced free verse and Communist themes to Turkish poetry in the 1920s. Because of his ideology he spent many years in Turkish prisons and fled his native country in 1951. He lived in the Soviet Union and Eastern Europe until his death in 1963. In addition to his voluminous poetry, he published novels, political columns, essays, plays, and movie scripts. His influence on Turkish poetry and leftist ideologies has been extensive. Hikmet's poetry has been translated into numerous major and minor languages throughout the world. He received many awards including the Lenin Peace Prize which he shared with Pablo Neruda in 1950. In Turkey he is known as Nazım Hikmet, referred to as Nazım for short; outside of Turkey, Hikmet is often employed as his last name. His official surname in Turkey was Ran, which he virtually never used in his publications.

ATTİLÂ İLHAN (1925–2005) was one of Turkey's most versatile and popular literary figures. He was a poet, novelist, essayist and critic, columnist, scriptwriter, and television personality. İlhan published scores of books of poetry and prose, including translations and travel writing.

ÖZDEMİR İNCE (1936–) is a prolific poet whose work as critic, essayist, columnist, and translator has also attracted considerable attention. He has worked as a teacher of French, scriptwriter and producer for Turkish TV, and editor at two publishing houses. He writes a weekly column for Turkey's largest circulation newspaper *Hürriyet.* He is a member of the Mallarmé Academy (Paris). In 2006 he was awarded the Max Jacob Prize (France) for his poetry.

ORHAN VELİ KANIK (1914–1950) was a major innovator and remains one of the most popular Turkish poets. His translations from the French and his essays also enjoy wide fame. His selected poems have been published in German and English versions.

CEYHUN ATUF KANSU (1919–1978) was a prolific poet and essayist who also turned out many children's books. A graduate of the Faculty of Medicine at the University of Istanbul, he worked many years as a pediatrician. He also held various posts at the Turkish Language Society.

NECİP FAZIL KISAKÜREK (1905–1983) was and remains one of Turkey's most controversial poets and writers because of his reactionary religious stance. In addition to many volumes of poetry, he published several volumes of memoirs, novels, collections of short stories, and dozens of collections of essays and journalistic articles. In the 1930s and 1940s he was a highly successful playwright. He was the editor in chief of the conservative Islamic periodical *Büyük Doğu* (Great Orient).

CAHİT KÜLEBİ (1917–1997) taught literature, served as Turkey's educational attaché in Switzerland, and was an assistant undersecretary for cultural affairs. In addition to eight books of poetry, he published a collection of essays and his memoirs. He served as editor in chief and secretary general of the Turkish Language Society for many years.

MURATHAN MUNGAN (1955–) enjoys fame as a widely admired poet, novelist, short-story writer, and playwright. He holds undergraduate and graduate degrees from the Department of Drama at Ankara University.

BEHÇET NECATİGİL (1916–1979) spent his entire working life as a high school literature teacher. His many books of poetry are notable for their unique poetic aesthetics. Although receptive to the spirit and expressive devices of the Ottoman classical tradition, the poetic synthesis he forged constituted one of the most original modernizing forces in Turkish verse. Necatigil is also renowned for his radio plays and his translations from German literature.

ÜMİT YAŞAR OĞUZCAN (1926–1984). A prolific poet, he enjoyed great popularity in his lifetime and in the years following his death. He also compiled numerous popular anthologies.

AHMET OKTAY (1933–) is one of Turkey's most prominent essayists and literary critics. He worked many years as a journalist and newspaper editor. For his poetry he has won a number of important awards.

İSMET ÖZEL (1944–) holds a degree in French language and literature and has worked as a teacher of French, as a government employee, and as publisher-editor. One of the most talented of his generation, he has been a controversial figure politically, switching from Communism to reactionary Islam.

KEMAL ÖZER (1935–) is a prolific poet and children's writer. He has also done some notable translations from a variety of languages. In addition to his lyric verse, he is well known for his poetry of social realism. He has been the editor of many important literary magazines.

OKTAY RİFAT (1914–1988), a major literary figure, graduated from the Faculty of Law at Ankara University and spent three years at the Sorbonne but returned to Turkey without completing his Ph.D. For many years he served as legal counsel for the Turkish State Railways. Rifat was one of the three major figures of the movement known as "Garip" (Strange) in the 1940s. From the mid-1950s onward he went through periods of obscurantism and philosophical verse. In addition to being one of Turkey's foremost modernists in poetry, he enjoyed renown as a playwright, novelist, and translator. He was honored with virtually all of Turkey's major literary awards.

SENNUR SEZER (1943–) has worked many years for newspapers, literary magazines, publishing houses, and radio and TV. In addition to numerous collections of poetry, she has published children's fiction, anthologies, collections of essays, and books on Ottoman culture, including a partly fictitious biography of the Ottoman woman poet Mihri Hatun (d. 1506).

CEMAL SÜREYA (1931–1990) is recognized as a major figure of modern Turkish literature—a revolutionary poet, a provocative critic and essayist, and a highly successful translator. A graduate of the Faculty of Political Science, Ankara University, he spent some years as an inspector of the Ministry of Finance and director of the Istanbul Mint. Süreya served as editor of several influential literary magazines. He was the recipient of some of Turkey's major awards.

ÜLKÜ TAMER (1937–) is an award-winning poet, short-story writer, and translator. He is currently a weekly columnist for the newspaper *Sabah.* He has also published numerous children's books and major anthologies. His scores of translations range from Euripides to Neil Simon, from Shakespeare to Brecht.

AHMET HAMDİ TANPINAR (1901–1962) achieved prominence as poet, novelist and short-story writer, essayist, translator, and literary scholar. Few other scholars are comparable to him in stature as a historian and critic of Turkey's intellectual and literary modernization. In the field of fiction, he is generally regarded as having wielded a profound influence. For many years Tanpınar was a professor at the Faculty of Literature at the University of Istanbul. He served one term as a member of Parliament.

CAHİT SITKI TARANCI (1910–1956). One of Turkey's best-loved lyricists, Tarancı worked as a translator for various government agencies. His poetry is collected in numerous volumes.

TURGUT UYAR (1927–1985) was one of the protagonists of the 1950s poetic movement that came to be known as the "Second New." For his poetry he was awarded some of Turkey's major prizes.

HİLMİ YAVUZ (1936–). A prominent poet who has incorporated into his work many of the aesthetic values of classical poetry, he has published many critically acclaimed volumes of poetry, collections of essays and articles, and translations. He studied philosophy at the University of London and taught philosophy at Istanbul's Boğaziçi and Mimar Sinan Universities. Currently he teaches modern Turkish literature at Ankara's Bilkent University.

CAN YÜCEL (1926–1999) was a living legend who published avant-garde poems, widely popular satiric verses, and creative translations, most of which paid little attention to fidelity. He studied briefly at Cambridge University, served in Korea as a reserve officer, lived for some years in Paris and London where he worked for the BBC. He contributed scores of articles and columns to newspapers and magazines. His translations, many of them renowned, include Shakespeare's *Hamlet, The Tempest,* and *A Midsummer-Night's Dream,* Scott Fitzgerald's *The Great Gatsby,* and Charles Dickens's *Oliver Twist.*

CAHİT ZARİFOĞLU (1940–1987), a graduate of the Department of German Language and Literature, the University of Istanbul, was a modernist who incorporated into his work the sensibilities, poetic devices, and the vernacular of classical Ottoman poetry with Islamic features. In addition to his collections of poetry, he published short stories, a novel, a play, children's books, and a collection of essays.

About the Editors

TALAT S. HALMAN is a leading translator of Turkish literature into English. His books in English include *Contemporary Turkish Literature, Modern Turkish Drama, Süleyman the Magnificent Poet,* three volumes on Yunus Emre, *Mevlana Celaleddin Rumi and the Whirling Dervishes* (with Metin And), *Shadows of Love* (his original poems in English), *A Last Lullaby* (his English/Turkish poems), *Living Poets of Turkey, Turkish Legends and Folk Poems,* and many books featuring modern Turkish poets (Dağlarca, Kanık, Anday) and playwrights (Güngör Dilmen, Cahit Atay, Dinçer Sümer). He was also editor of *A Dot on the Map: Selected Stories and Poems by Sait Faik, Sleeping in the Forest: Stories and Poems* by Sait Faik, and *Nightingales and Pleasure Gardens: Turkish Love Poems,* the last two books published by Syracuse University Press. *ForeWord Reviews* named *Nightingales and Pleasure Gardens* one of the ten best university press books of 2005.

Among his books in Turkish are ten collections of his own poetry, a massive volume of the poetry of ancient civilizations, the complete sonnets of Shakespeare, the poetry of ancient Anatolia and the Near East, Eskimo poems, ancient Egyptian poetry, the *rubai*s of Rumi, the quatrains of Baba Tahir Uryan, two anthologies of modern American poetry, and books of the selected poems of Wallace Stevens and Langston Hughes. He was William Faulkner's first Turkish translator; he also translated Mark Twain and Eugene O'Neill.

Halman has published nearly 3,000 articles, essays, newspaper columns, and reviews in English and in Turkish. Some of his books have been translated into French, German, Hebrew, Persian, Urdu, Hindi, and Japanese. For his work as a translator he won Columbia University's Thornton Wilder Prize.

Talat Halman served as Turkey's first minister of culture and later as its ambassador for cultural affairs; he was a member of the Executive Board of UNESCO. Currently, he is president of the Turkish National Committee for UNICEF. Between 1953 and 1997 he was on the faculties of Columbia University, Princeton University, the University of Pennsylvania, and New York University (where he also was chairman of the Department of Near Eastern Languages and Literatures). In 1998 he founded the Department of Turkish Literature at Bilkent University, Ankara, and has since served as its chairman. He is also Bilkent's dean of the Faculty of Humanities and Letters. He is editor in chief of the *Journal of Turkish Studies* and general editor for a four-volume history of Turkish literature to be published in Turkish.

In 2001 Dr. Jayne L. Warner compiled and edited a Festschrift in his honor titled *Cultural Horizons* (Syracuse University Press/Yapı Kredi Yayınları). This two-volume work consists of seventy-two articles by prominent scholars, authors, and statesmen and contains a comprehensive bibliography of Halman's work. His honors and awards include many literary prizes, an honorary doctorate, a Rockefeller Fellowship in the Humanities, the Distinguished Service Award of the Turkish Academy of Sciences, the UNESCO Medal, and Knight Grand Cross (GBE), "The Most Excellent Order of the British Empire," conferred on him by Queen Elizabeth II.

JAYNE L. WARNER is director of research at the Institute for Aegean Prehistory in Greenwich, Connecticut. She holds a B.A. in classics, an M.A. in ancient history and, from Bryn Mawr College, a Ph.D. in Near Eastern and Anatolian archaeology. Her publications include *Elmalı-Karataş II: The Early Bronze Age Village of Karataş*. Warner has served as assistant editor of the American School of Classical Studies in Athens and executive director of the Poetry Society of America (New York). She has also served as director of the American Turkish Society (New York) and director of the office of the Board of Trustees of Robert College of Istanbul. She was the editor of *Cultural Horizons: A Festschrift in Honor of Talat S. Halman* and associate editor of *Sleeping in the Forest: Stories and Poems* by Sait Faik and *Nightingales and Pleasure Gardens: Turkish Love Poems,* all three published by Syracuse University Press.

Acknowledgments

The editors offer their thanks to Türkiye İş Bankası Kültür Yayınları and to the following individuals for their assistance with various aspects of the production of this book: Yusuf Alphan Akgül, Ceyda Akpolat, Suna Anday, Günil Özlem Ayaydın Cebe, Demet Güzelsoy Chafra, Doğan Hızlan, Mustafa Şerif Onaran, İlknur Özdemir, Ela Şengündüz, Ali Kemal Temizer, Baran Tuncer, and Erol Ulu.

Also the editors are grateful to the following publishers for permission to reprint these translations by Talat S. Halman: *The Literary Review* 15, no. 4 (1972) (Special Issue, ed. Talat S. Halman): Melih Cevdet Anday, "Copper Age"; Ceyhan Atuf Kansu, "The Critics"; Turgut Uyar, "And Came the Tailors." *Literature East & West* 13, nos. 3–4 (December 1969): Orhan Veli Kanık, "Living" and "For Our Homeland"; 17, no. 1 (March 1973) (Special Issue, ed. Talat S. Halman): Melih Cevdet Anday, "On the Nomad Sea"; Salâh Birsel, "Geography Lesson"; Fazıl Hüsnü Dağlarca, "Audience" and "A Corpse Turns Cold"; Ahmet Muhip Dıranas, "Have and Have Not [Two Solitary Trees]"; Nazım Hikmet, "Today Is Sunday"; Ümit Yaşar Oğuzcan, "The Left Ear of the Grand Vizier"; Ülkü Tamer, "The Dagger." *Modern Poetry in Translation,* First Series, no. 10 (Spring 1971): Attilâ İlhan, "Ancient Sea Folk." *the new renaissance* 6, no. 1 (Spring 1984): Ahmet Erhan, "Waiting Beside a Friend's Coffin"; Cemal Süreya, "Just at These Hours."